Can You Hear God?

Joyce Sibthorpe

New Wine Press

New Wine Press
PO Box 17
Chichester
West Sussex
PO20 6YB
England

Copyright © 1995 Joyce Sibthorpe

All rights reserved. No part of this publication may be
reproduced, stored in a retrieval system, or transmitted, in any
form or by any means, electronic, mechanical, photocopying,
recording or otherwise, without the prior written consent of the
publisher.

Short extracts may be used for review purposes.

Scripture quotations are taken from the HOLY BIBLE,
New International Version. Copyright © 1973, 1978, 1984
by International Bible Society. Used by permission.

ISBN: 1 874367 41 8

Cover design: David Salmon.
Typeset by CRB Associates, Norwich.
Printed in England by Clays Ltd, St Ives plc.

Acknowledgements

I want to express my thanks to those who have helped in the production of this book. First, to Anne Vyce who transcribed the original spoken messages which provided the basis of the book, and undertook the word processing; my husband Charles who worked on the early draft manuscript, and in particular Alison Kember who gave me great help in making sure that the text was really communicating the intentions of the book.

Contents

Foreword

I am delighted to recommend this book on hearing
God. Joyce has been a friend for many years since she
and her husband, Charles, came to work with Colin
and me in the mid-seventies. I have been blessed and
encouraged through her and value her warm friend-
ship.

Joyce is a very practical person and her questioning
mind has opened the way for God to teach her many
things. In this book, she shares very openly her walk
with God over the years. She clearly and sensitively
explains the 'how to' of listening to God's voice. Both
new Christians and the more mature will be *encouraged in developing a listening ear* to God and increase
their relationship with Him.

I believe this is a timely book for the body of
Christ, as God is pouring out His Holy Spirit in
abundance and He is urging us to hear the voice of
the Holy Spirit so that we can go into the nation,
following His instruction to extend the Kingdom of
God in our land. Jesus could do nothing without the
Father; so the same applies to us. It is of the utmost

importance that we increase our ability to hear His voice. So I pray that all who read this book will grow into a deeper *relationship* with God, hearing Him more clearly.

Caroline Urquhart

Chapter 1

A Matter of Life or Death

I was out in the garden when the telephone rang; I raced inside to pick it up and to my surprise it was the local hospital. They were ringing, very concerned, about a young woman with whom we'd had a great deal of contact over the previous two years. She had been a regular baby-sitter in our family and was a young woman with great emotional needs. She'd gone to the hospital for a routine chest X-ray, but whilst there fear had overcome her to such an extent that the hospital were contemplating sending her to the local mental hospital because she was so out of control. She'd told the hospital to contact us saying, 'These people know me, they understand me, please ring them and they'll come and get me.' The ultimatum from the hospital was 'either you come immediately and pick this girl up because she's absolutely out of control, or we put her in an ambulance and take her up to the local mental hospital.' I put the 'phone down, rang Charles who was at work in the town; he came back and collected me and together we went up to the hospital. Fortunately we had someone in the house to look after the children. We didn't want to take this young woman back into our family situation because it was school holidays. There were four little children at home, and this was no place to take someone who was severely distraught. So we went to the home of Di and Mark, a young couple belonging to our church, who were very good friends of ours. They had recently moved into a new bungalow with plenty of space and peace and quiet where we felt we could minister to this young woman.

I can't remember now whether we rang them or simply 'landed' on them, but we said to them 'you pray – just sit in another room and pray whilst we minister to this young woman.' They were agreeable with that as they also wanted to see her set free because she was a very good friend to all of us.

Some weeks before this incident Jean Darnall had been visiting our home and speaking in the locality. We had asked Jean to minister to this young woman but again the fear, or the terror, as Jean discerned it to be, just rose up and she was unable to minister to her. Jean's parting remark as she left our home had been, 'you have got her trust and you two will have to minister deliverance to her.' And so here it was. We were very, very inexperienced. We knew that God was powerful and that He wanted to deliver people from fear and terror and every manifestation of demonic, satanic forces. But in terms of experience we had never ministered in this way before. We knew, too, that we needed to cover all the people in the household from any danger that might come. We prayed, asking the Lord to cover every person in the house with His blood and to protect us from anything evil. I think in those days we were probably somewhat afraid of the devil and had less understanding of the almighty power of God.

So tentatively we prayed, asking God to cover the house in the blood of Jesus and every person in it. As we were sitting quietly, about to minister to her the Lord spoke to my heart and He said, 'pray for the unborn child.' Immediately I retorted inside myself, 'but there isn't one.' There was no unborn child, as far as I knew, inside that house. But again the voice of the Holy Spirit came very urgently and very insistently, 'pray for the unborn child.' So I quietly prayed, 'Lord, cover the unborn child that is in this house with your blood.' We then began to pray and minister deliverance to the young woman concerned.

God set her free. He set her gloriously free – she knew it and we knew it and we were rejoicing. After the hugs and the tears were over I said to the other couple who had now come back in the room, 'are you by any chance pregnant?' 'No' was the reply 'not us.' As I walked back down the road to our own home I thought, 'well, it must be me then.' I didn't think I was pregnant, I wasn't expecting to be and it would have taken at least two weeks before I would have known that. But in fact, less than two weeks later, the friend who I'd asked came to me and said, 'I am pregnant and I must have only conceived just a few days before you ministered in our house when God directed you to pray for that unborn child.' Now I was absolutely amazed by that; I shouldn't have been because in the Bible we read that God spoke to Jeremiah and said *'even before you were formed I knew you.'* And God certainly knew the baby that at that point had been conceived and was growing in the womb of our friend.

Less than six weeks later that same friend contracted German measles and was asked to have an abortion. The doctor told her that she was very young with many years ahead of her when she could have children, she hadn't had the anti-German measles jab so consequently it was better to be safe than sorry and to have a termination. So she and her husband were faced with this awful decision of being told this by the medical authorities and yet knowing that God had seen this baby, probably at two or three days of conception when I had prayed specifically for its protection. In the light of that they decided that they would not have the pregnancy terminated and that she would carry this baby and trust that as the Lord had spoken in such a way the baby was safe. I'm glad to be able to say that the baby, a boy named Luke, was born perfectly healthy, perfectly normal, and an exceptionally beautiful child. He's just completed the second year of a degree at Cambridge; anointed of God academically, musically, very gifted with languages and called by God to serve the Lord full-time in Finland.

I just want to say that the ability to hear God saved his life. If the Lord had not spoken and if we had not prayed for his safety it might well have been that the pressure would have been too great and he could have been aborted; that was the sensible thing to do. But God had His hand on him, that is why God spoke about him and the preciousness of his life. I'm so thankful that I heard the voice of God and that saved a life.

I want to encourage everybody who is going to read this book to really become an expert, to seek to hear the voice of God, because it could be a matter of life or death.

Chapter 2

Let's Start Simply

'Can you hear God?' – this is the question around which this book revolves. Whatever may be your response at this moment, by the time you finish, I pray your answer will be a resounding 'Yes'.

When I started preparing this book, I asked God a question: 'at what level should I begin, Lord?' His reply was, 'start simply; be honest, be open, share what you have.'

When Peter came to that man at the Gate Beautiful (you will find it in the book of the Acts chapter 3), he said,

> 'Silver and gold I do not have, but what I have I give you.'

In the same way I say, 'what I have, what I've learnt, I want to give to you.' You can take it and use it, but don't stop where I take you, go on, because there is so much more. Listening to God is a topic that can never be exhausted; there is always more; you always feel you are only beginning, but you need to start.

Developing your ability to listen to the voice of God will become such an exciting adventure.

Hearing from God is not wishful thinking, it is based on God's promises. Proverbs 8:34 says

> *'Blessed is the man who listens to me, watching daily at my doors, waiting at my doorway. For whoever finds me finds life and receives favour from the Lord.'*

This is the promise which can release you to seriously listen to God. So, if you want to find favour from the Lord, then you will become someone who daily listens. This will bless, prosper and enrich you in spirit, and that's good news.

There is an agony in the heart of God as He searches for those who will listen to His voice. This is expressed poignantly in Jeremiah 6:10,

> *'To whom can I speak and give warning? Who will listen to me? Their ears are closed so that they cannot hear. The Word of the LORD is offensive to them; they find no pleasure in it.'*

As I read that I find myself saying, 'Oh God, I know how You feel; it's a terrible thing when you are trying to explain something to a friend, knowing you are using your common language, and yet everything you see is telling you that they're not hearing you. It's so frustrating, because you can't communicate to that person what's in your heart. They can hear the words with their physical ears, they appear to be listening, but they are not receiving what you are saying and there is something of an agony in your spirit, particularly if you are trying to share something which is deep and intimate.'

That's the heart of God. He is saying, 'to whom can I speak and give warning? Who will listen to me? Their ears are closed.' Now the Prophet is talking about the children of Israel, but I believe the Spirit of God is in fact seeking to share the agony of His heart with you and me.

That word 'closed' actually means 'uncircumcised'. Now circumcision makes something very, very sensitive. God talks constantly about the children of Israel having 'uncircumcised hearts' which meant that they were hardened, they weren't sensitized, they hadn't had the outer covering removed so that they became very tender and sensitive. An alternative reading would be 'their ears are uncircumcised'. I believe that God wants to do that to our ears; take the covering off them, make them sensitive. If that is what you want, ask Him now. 'Please Lord, circumcise my ears, let them become sensitive to Your voice.'

Think of the distress in Stephen's heart as he addressed the Sanhedrin in Acts 7:51. Again, it's an agony verse; Stephen is speaking, anointed by the Holy Spirit, just before they stone him to death. He has preached his heart out to the Israeli people and now says:

> *'You stiff-necked people, with uncircumcised hearts and ears! You are just like your fathers: you always resist the Holy Spirit.'*

There it is again, 'uncircumcised heart', 'uncircumcised ears'. I don't want to be like that, nor do you; we want God to say 'these people have had their ears circumcised, so that they are open.' That's our desire, isn't it? The Lord wants to give us our desires; if you are prepared to say 'I want to hear you Lord' then He is already on your side; He wants to bless you, He wants to open your ears, He wants to give you a confidence in hearing him.

Do you know how to hear?

This is the key question. You will need to answer that question affirmatively, if you are to make progress.

There is a difference between the transient: 'Yes I hear God, I have heard God on occasions' and the more permanent: 'I know how to hear Him.' I know that if I were to say 'have you heard God?' many readers would be able to reply, 'yes, I have.' But if I asked you 'do you hear God on a regular ongoing basis?' you would probably be a little more tentative in your response.

God wants to take us from 'yes, I do on occasions' to 'yes, I can.' Half the battle, when you are learning anything, is knowing you can do it.

This was the situation with our daughter, Coralie, some years ago, when she was about 13 or 14. She had listened to some teaching that I had given at a Faith Camp on this subject, and she said to herself, 'Mum told me I could hear God, she told me I could do it, and she told me to get a notebook and actually to write down in it what I hear; so I will.'

She was also encouraged by a prophecy given at this time through which God spoke concerning her ears, saying they would become very sensitive to His voice. So she thought, 'I'd better start using them.'

Then for two years, quite unbeknown to me, she

had been doing this – simply because she had been told 'you can.' One evening there was a power cut, and she could not continue her school work, so we began to talk in the candlelight. Charles and I were facing a decision that would bring drastic changes into our lives, and we were undecided as to the right course of action. As the conversation drifted to this subject Coralie suddenly said, 'do you want to know what God has said to me about this?' 'I certainly do', was my stunned reply. So off she went to get her note-book, and crouching over the candle she read out just the confirmation Charles and I were needing. And this was our teenage daughter.

I want to tell you, '**You** can hear God's voice.' Jesus said *'My sheep hear My voice.'* **You** can do it, it's the enemy who has told you all these years that you can't. Although you might get it wrong some of the time, once you know that you can hear, then you will do it, and as you continue doing it you will grow in confidence and accuracy.

'But He doesn't speak to us to-day'

I became a Christian when I was 11, and with no religious background at all, I had none of the teaching which says, 'you don't do it this way.' The lady who led me to a personal faith in Jesus was very wise when I told her I didn't know how to pray. It was not only not knowing how to pray, I hadn't got a clue what prayer was. By way of explanation, she placed a chair in the middle of the room and another one alongside and said, 'you sit down there,' so I sat on it, and then she said 'now, God is in that chair,' pointing to the vacant chair beside me, 'now tell Him everything.

You can't see Him, but He is there.' So I learnt to pray, believing there was a real person sitting beside me who was interested in what I was telling Him, and He got the lot! If I was happy, He got it; if I was sad and moaning and angry He got that as well. But I was so thankful for that instruction and counsel, because I realised that I was developing a relationship with a person. I couldn't see Him but I knew He was my Father, I knew He cared about me, I knew He was interested in me and many times I unburdened all my pent up anger on to Him, at other times I told Him the joys that were in my heart. But I also expected Him to speak to me, because in any human relationship there must be two-way communication. So my expectation was that He would speak and because of that I was listening.

Now, God is wonderfully gracious; I was a young girl of 11 years old, He was my Father, He was real to me and I expected Him to help me. In fact, I had come to God because I cried out to Him, 'I need a Father.' I didn't have a Father in human terms (my parents had divorced when I was only 4 years old), so when I knew that God actually wanted to be my Father, that He was my Father and accepted me, it was a wonderful feeling. He was someone who was for me, was on my side, would defend me, would help me.

At the time I came to a living faith in Jesus, I was in a boarding school which had many extremely 'petty' rules and restrictions. On a Monday and Wednesday morning we used to have to put our laundry in various baskets. It was pants in this basket, hankies over here, socks there, and somebody would tick off the list. I now understand you need those sort of rules when you have 400 people living in a boarding school situation where everybody needs to have the right things at the right time. I was a scatty child as well as a rebel, and never had all that was required at this crucial moment; but having been converted, I was now trying to be good. I can remember thinking, 'I've got my pants and I've got my socks ... Uuuuuuh, Where's my hanky?!'

Now I can laugh, but at the time it was a crisis of monumental proportions; I was going to get in trouble yet again for not having all the required items. I remember going down into the basement of the dormitory house building and looking in all my pockets trying to find a handkerchief, so that I could get my 'tick'. I checked every pocket without success and I was beginning to feel desperate. I was really trying to live out my new found faith and here I was breaking the rules straightaway! Then I heard it, a voice within. It was the Spirit of God saying to me, 'go and look in your outside coat pocket.' It wasn't from outside me, nobody else heard it, yet I heard it clearly. I can remember arguing and saying, 'I've already looked down there' but the voice inside was insistent: 'go and look again.' So I went back into the basement, felt in my outside coat pocket and there was the handkerchief. That for me was a miracle! I think God must have instructed an angel to fish around all my belongings and find the handkerchief. It had my number on it too, '356', and in it went.

It sounds so simple, but you see, God is concerned with little practical things as well as big spiritual things, and that was the first time I could really say I heard the voice of God and became excited about it, and began telling people 'do you know what God did for me? He really did.'

But, unfortunately, my traditional and entrenched Christian friends said 'no dear, He doesn't do it like that today. He only speaks to you through the Bible,' and so my expectancy of hearing God personally was crushed. I started to hear Him through the Word of God, reading my Bible, and He did speak to me, but I stopped hearing that intimate Father's voice – because I lost the expectancy when I was told 'He doesn't do it that way today.'

But you need to know that 'He does do it that way today.' To each one of us He is our Father, He is the Holy Spirit within us. He wants to communicate regularly to us all, deeply, into every area of life, and He wants to train us to hear His voice, whether it's personal, practical things or whether it's a prophetic word as we lay hands on someone. He wants to train us and nobody is left out. If God can speak to me and open my ears, He can speak to you and open your ears, because we are all His sheep, we are no different from each other.

There are no disadvantaged people in the Kingdom of God. There are no victims in the Kingdom of God. There are many victims in this world, many people who have been victimised by the circumstances of life, but in the Kingdom of God we all have the same resources and the same advantages.

Sadly, I did not continue as I had begun. The years rolled by and although it would not be true to say that I never heard the voice of God, traditional religious thought had all but silenced that simple, fresh and exciting communication with my heavenly Father; but that was about to change. The Spirit of God was moving, and the hunger in my heart for a greater intimacy with God was growing. Eventually we were invited to attend a conference in Ireland where God met with Charles and me in the power of His Holy Spirit. Immediately hands were laid on us to receive the Holy Spirit, the voice of the Spirit was re-awakened within me. He began to speak about many areas that needed cleansing. He spoke about books I had read that did not glorify God and needed to be destroyed – they glorified Satan not God. And He reminded me of incidents which again He was not pleased with, and I needed to ask for forgiveness and cleansing.

We spent hours on our knees asking for forgiveness for everything that the Spirit of God convicted us of. He was very specific and so were we!

Chapter 3

Make Listening a Daily Routine

Now I was filled with the Holy Spirit, this time of silence had come to an end. Once more He was getting through to me and telling me specific things.

I am reminded of a situation which occurred on a ferry boat returning from Ireland. I was coming back from the conference centre where I had been filled with the Holy Spirit, and I simply felt in need of peace and quiet. I had my third child, a three-month-old son, on the boat with me. I was enjoying having him in my arms at the end of a week when so much of spiritual significance had happened, and was settling down for a night crossing of the Irish Sea back to Liverpool to pick up our car and go back home to Cornwall. It had been a busy week, and I was digesting all that we had heard when quietly but very insistently the Holy Spirit said to me, 'go and sit beside that woman over there.' My immediate response was to resist the words I was hearing.

I know only too well my natural reflex action; my instinctive nature is always to argue, though the Lord was and is training me and trying to teach me not to be rebellious. I said 'no, no, no!' but that inner voice was insistent, and I knew the Lord was saying 'go and sit over there.' Eventually, after quite a lot of hesitation and inner struggle, I went and sat next to this lady. We exchanged the normal greetings and courtesies, and she responded by saying to me 'do you want a cup of tea?', producing a flask. I quickly replied, 'yes, that would be lovely, thank you.' A conversation began; I asked her what she did, and she told me that she worked in a mental hospital. Quite spontaneously and without a lot of thought, I found myself saying to her 'does anybody ever get healed?' She looked at me with venom and the explosion that followed was unbelievable, out of all proportion to what I had said!

'Nobody gets healed today, nobody gets healed,' she said to me, to which I replied, 'oh yes, they do.' She retorted, 'no, they don't!' and continued angrily, 'you show me somebody who has been healed.' I was ready to respond to this question! About 20 minutes before the boat had set out to cross the Irish Sea, I had had the most chronic stomach-ache and a real pain under my diaphragm; I knew I had a night crossing ahead, and had gone up on deck to take a breath of air when I heard God say to me, 'lay your hands on yourself, rebuke this pain and tell it to go and I'll heal you.' I had done it, which was the first time I had ever done anything like that, and the pain had gone immediately. I was still rejoicing to be free of it. So I could testify to this lady, 'I was healed. It took place about half an hour ago,' and I gave her the details.

Almost at once she began to cry, tears coming from deep within her. Then her story began tumbling out. She had been trained in a Roman Catholic Order, but when she was diagnosed as having a brain tumour the religious order to which she belonged sent her home to her village, which was in Southern Ireland, to die; but miraculously God had healed her.

Subsequently, the war came and she had not gone back to her Order, but had moved to Birmingham. She had worked as a nurse, got married, and as the years had passed by had lost touch with God and with her faith. God was no longer a dimension in her life. Then I came onto the boat, sat opposite her and awoke everything within that woman which spoke of God and her past, all quite unbeknown to me.

It was a divine appointment, and particularly concerning the healing. She knew she couldn't deny that she had been healed, and the encounter had a wonderful outcome. She came back to the Lord, her faith in God was restored, and at the end of the journey we exchanged addresses and for many years we remained in contact.

I'm so glad that God spoke and I was obedient, even if after a struggle, because He knows what He is doing. We just need to be obedient to what we hear and do it, because there is always great fruit and I know the excitement I felt at being directed by the Spirit of God into such a situation.

One of the reasons why I had wanted to be baptised in the Spirit was because I wanted power. I had constantly felt so totally inadequate when witnessing to people. I knew all the procedures but was scared stiff in case I missed a step out which might prevent somebody properly entering into the Kingdom of God. Now, suddenly, God had shown me I didn't need to worry; I didn't need to 'get it all right', I just needed to listen to His voice, be obedient to what He said and become involved in the situation He had set up. Here it was happening to me and through me, 'what I have, I give you.' What you have you can give to the people that God puts in your pathway.

I could relate a number of these kinds of situations, but I am sorry to have to admit they were not consistent. They were a kind of 'one off' and perhaps six months later something else would happen.

Making it 'regular'

It wasn't until I joined the Bethany Fellowship at the Hyde in Sussex that I saw a man who daily sat at the feet of Jesus and made a record of what he had heard. Our daily pattern of life began with a morning prayer time when the whole team would gather to worship the Lord, listen to Him and prepare for the day ahead. We met each day in the Library which was filled with valuable books, a rich blue carpet on the floor and a pink chair. If we went into the room early, Colin Urquhart would be sitting in the pink chair with his notebook and he would be writing away. I am naturally very inquisitive, so 'nosey' me came along and asked 'what are you doing?' His reply was 'I'm just listening to the Lord.'

I said, 'what? You just sit there every day and listen to God?'

'Yes, I read my Bible, I pray, but I always spend some time every day simply with my notebook writing down what the Lord says.'

That absolutely blew my mind. It had never entered my head to do something like that consistently each day, but as a team he encouraged us to follow his example.

It was not long before I had purchased my own notebook and began listening each day. I remember feeling very foolish after completing my first piece, I looked at it and thought I had made it up, closed the book and began to pray for my family. However the next morning when I looked at what I had written I was amazed because I could see clearly that God had spoken; He had given me words of encouragement and direction for the past day. Encouraged by this, I persevered with this 'writing down in a note book' and I knew after a while that God was beginning to speak to me, but I was insecure. I wasn't confident at all. If I had been asked the question that I asked you at the beginning 'can you hear God?' I would have probably been one of those people who said 'no,' even though I know I could. In fact I wasn't secure enough to say 'yes, I can.'

The practice of listening pivots on the ability to tune in to the voice of God. Listening to the voice of the Lord is like a musician listening to an orchestra; each musician will pick out the sound of the instrument with which he is most familiar. Have you noticed that? If you're a flute player, you'll be very conscious of the flute part in the piece that's being performed. If you're a pianist, all sorts can be going on but you'll be listening to the piano because your ear is tuned to that instrument. The more time you spend listening to the Lord, the more clearly you will hear his voice.

If you want to become a musician of any quality you have to practise scales, whether your instrument is the piano, the violin or something else. It's slog, it's routine, but it is vital to get the dexterity into your fingers. It's not particularly tuneful, you just do it. I see the daily writing down, listening to God on a daily basis, as just that same discipline of playing scales. You are training yourself to listen and because you are training your ear, when God needs to speak you can hear; you have the sensitivity you need to hear when He wants you to do a job.

There are conflicting voices however. There is the voice of the accuser as well as the voice of the Comforter. You need to learn to distinguish between the two. Because the accuser always wants to put you down, any negative, undermining voice will be the devil. Right at the start he'll say: 'you're not hearing God, you're making it up. What a load of nonsense. Don't do that, hearing God is only for the special people. Who do you think you are? Is God going to speak to you?' That's the voice of the enemy and he says that to all of us when we start.

But, remember: you know you are a child of God and His sheep hear His voice. In John 8:47 it says,

'He who belongs to God hears what God says.'

You belong to God so you can hear what He says. You have His Spirit in your heart which happened when you were born again. You are born by the Spirit of God and the Spirit of God is there inside you and He wants to come out, He wants to be released, He wants to speak to you, He wants you to open your ears.

So – if you mean business, go out and buy yourself a notebook and actually determine as a quality decision that you will get before God and you will listen on a daily basis. You have got to do it. God isn't going to drop a notebook from Heaven, you've got to go out and buy one, you've got to decide 'I'm here, Lord, I'm going to be trained by You, I'm going to do it.'

Chapter 4

Preparing the Ground

During the time we were part of the Bethany Fellowship (now Kingdom Faith Ministries) and living at the
Hyde, John Wimber came to London and I attended
what must have been one of the first Conferences he
held in London. During the ministry time, which he
used to call 'clinic', two of his team came towards me.
I thought they were coming to the young man sitting
next to me, a member of the fellowship who lived in
our home, who as the result of a motor bike accident
could not bend his leg. I was almost calling them over,
interfering by saying 'he's here, he's here. Come and
pray for him.' But they said 'no, God isn't asking us
to pray for him, He's asking us to pray for you.'

One of the young men took hold of my hands and
said 'These hands have been busy hands. These hands
have been hard-working hands. God is not pleased
with you because you have been so busy "doing" that
you haven't sat at His feet and listened.'

I felt shamed and overwhelmed with sadness,
because I knew it was the truth. I had been so busy
'doing' that I hadn't spent any time listening. I had
been working in my own strength, rather than in the

strength of The Holy Spirit, and consequently had almost reached a point of exhaustion. They continued to hover around me, as is their pattern of ministry, but I had heard the Word of the Lord and simply wanted to say, 'Just clear off and leave me alone, I need to listen to God!'

When they had gone I sat there as the tears flowed. I repented first of all and confessed the sin in my life that I'd become too busy for God. Then I said, 'well, Lord, speak to me.' I rummaged through my handbag to find something to write on, and this is what He said: 'I want you to lay aside everything. I want you to give me a clean piece of paper. I want to tell you what I want you to do. You're so busy in so many areas, but have you asked Me whether you should be involved? Draw aside and listen to Me.'

Find the space!

When faced with an emergency you drop everything to do what is necessary. God spoke with such urgency that I knew my life depended on obedience. I went home and asked to be released from every responsibility that could be described as non-essential. My actions were not always understood but I knew at this time God's voice demanded I spent time with Him and so I **made** space. You will have to make space, make time. It will never just happen. It's not easy at home, in your normal life situation, to seek the Lord, is it? Every time I say to myself 'I'm going to spend some time listening to the Lord and seeking Him,' I think 'I'll do the dishes first' and then I think, 'now, I'll put the washing in the washing machine, and then it'll be doing while I'm listening to the Lord,' and then I think, 'oh dear, the cat's bowl needs washing' and before I know where I am, I'm picking things up en-route, and if I'm not careful, I don't get to the Lord at all, because of all the practical daily chores. You never see cobwebs until you actually want to be quiet with the Lord and then there's a massive great cobweb; it's been there for ages, but you don't see it until you decide to go and spend time with the Lord. That's the enemy and we have to be aware of his devices.

So I booked Colin's study (he was away at the time) where I knew I could be quiet and shut the door, and I told everyone 'please don't disturb me for the next two hours.' It was good for me that there was such a room, but you have to find your own place where you can be quiet. It may be under a tree, it may be walking round the block, but you have to find somewhere where you are unimpeded by the ordinary daily tasks that scream out for your attention.

I walked into the study, sat down and as I began to worship the Lord I found myself singing a song. These are the words:

> 'Holy Spirit come, make my ears to hear,
> make my eyes to see,
> make my mouth to speak,
> make my heart to sing
> and my hands to reach out
> and touch the world with Your love.'

Make my ears to hear

It's an old song and I began to sing it over and over to the Lord, just waiting to hear what He had to say to me. I then clearly heard him say, 'this morning, we're going to deal with your ears.' He began to speak into my heart and said, 'what about those ears?' and I said 'well, Lord, I don't think I can really hear You,' and He said 'we're going to sort that out this morning. Put your hands on your ears, and in the same way as I commanded the ears of people in the New Testament to be opened, the physical ears, I want you now to take authority, put your fingers on your ears and command that they be opened, those inner ears, that they be opened in the Name of Jesus.'

I did just that. I felt quite foolish, but I did it, and God then said to me 'now, don't ever doubt that you can hear My voice again.' I look back to that time as a key point in my pilgrimage of learning to listen, as there have been many times when I have doubted, but when I think back to that moment I am always re-assured.

If you doubt that you can hear God – just get on your own, and take the authority that you have in Jesus and speak to those inner ears, those ears that can hear God and actually say 'be opened in the Name of Jesus.'

Write down in your notebook or record it some-where that on this day, at such and such a time, you commanded those ears to be opened and believe that the Spirit of God has opened them and you can hear. Do it.

Isaiah 50:4 and 5 says,

> *'The Sovereign* LORD *has given me an instructed tongue, to know the word that sustains the weary. He wakens me morning by morning, wakens my ear to listen like one being taught. The Sovereign*

LORD has opened my ears, and I have not been rebellious; I have not drawn back.'

That's what I am saying – The Sovereign Lord will open our ears. Ask in the Name of Jesus, for whatever you ask for in prayer, believe that you have received it, and it will be yours. You need to believe that when you ask the Sovereign Lord to open your ears, He's done it. Let there be no more arguing and saying 'I think I can hear' and then 'no, I don't think I can.' Confess you can hear, expect to hear and train that ear to listen daily and you'll hear the Lord.

But the Lord had not finished with me yet, the song I had sung was to be the blueprint for God to prepare me for a new dimension of being sensitive to His voice. I needed a thorough spring clean. At the end of the first morning He said to me, 'that's enough for today, next time we will deal with your eyes.'

I'll say more about that later.

Chapter 5

Jesus Shows us the Way

Jesus is our example in everything.

I don't know why, but I used to find the Gospels a bit boring. I quite liked Paul's letters, I loved the Old Testament, but there was a dull familiarity with the Gospels. It might have been that I'd heard them over and over again in Sunday School or as a child in RE lessons, but somehow or other I never found the Gospels brought me freshness or impact. It's taken me years to be able to read them and truly get excited about them. But recently I've been looking at the life of Jesus in a new way, in an exciting kind of way. For if I regard Him as the example for us to follow, which I believe is the basic aim of the Gospels, then I have to say: what He can do, He wants us to do. So I began to go through the Gospels with fresh eyes examining the way Jesus listened to and obeyed the will of His Father.

In John 12:49, Jesus says,

> *'I did not speak of my own accord, but the Father who sent me commanded me what to say and how to say it.'*

Jesus only said what the Father spoke to Him, He only did what the Father told Him to do. If Jesus needed to listen and obey the directions of His Father, how much more do we need to do it? I think that was the secret of how He could live His life in peace, joy and harmony without getting bogged down. He didn't heal everybody, even though He must have seen all the sickness amongst those who didn't come to Him and ask. He didn't deliver everybody, even though He must have been aware of all the demon possessed people around Him who hadn't come or who God hadn't pointed out to Him. He only did what the Father told Him to do. Leaders can suffer great stress and burden if they feel they have to respond to all the need that surrounds them. It's impossible to minister to every need. However, if we learn to hear the voice of the Lord, we'll do what He wants us to do.

Soaking in the Word

In order to be sensitive in hearing the voice of God we need to fill our minds and hearts with the right stuff. Jesus soaked Himself in the Word of God.

Listening to the voice of God in the way I have been describing is no substitute for us knowing the Bible, the written Word of God. In fact, you will not be able to discern the voice of God unless you know the Word of God. Hebrews 4:12 says:

> *'For the word of God is living and active. Sharper than any double edged sword, it penetrates even to dividing soul and spirit, joints and marrow; it judges the thoughts and attitudes of the heart.'*

The Word of God will establish a confidence in you that will help you to recognise the voice of God when you hear it. The Holy Spirit speaks with one voice, and He will never tell you anything which is contrary to Scripture. The more you know of the Scriptures, the easier it will be to recognise the speaking voice of God when you listen.

Do you remember when Jesus was aged twelve and he became separated from His parents? When they eventually found Him, He was talking with the teachers, the Scribes and the people in the temple who were amazed at His understanding and the way He knew the Scriptures. He was only twelve years old, but He had obviously read the Old Testament Scrolls. He had come to know the Word of God. Whether He spent a lot of time listening or talking to the older people in His own village in Nazareth, we don't know. But He knew the Word and it was deep in Him.

If you are going to be a person who listens to God you've got to get the Word of God into you. It has to be food for you. I am appalled at how many people, Christian people, who genuinely love the Lord, but are starving through lack of a good diet of the Word of God. They are like famine victims.

Once, when I was in Sweden, I was looking out on a congregation of people in one of the Swedish State Churches and had the most incredible vision. God showed me that I was in fact speaking to a whole group of emaciated people, all skin and bone and skulls. It was a frightening picture and I said 'Lord, what is it?' He said 'That's the true condition of My people because they are starving. They will not take My Word; they have it freely, they can use it, they can read it, it's food to them, but they are starving.' They are getting their snack on a Sunday – it's like eating a Mcdonald's hamburger once on a Sunday and nothing else for the rest of the week.

Hearing God 'loudly'

When Jesus came to His baptism at the time he was about to commence His ministry here on earth, He heard an audible voice from God, because at that moment He needed it. Jesus heard the voice of the Father speaking to Him in a way which was obviously quite different, quite significant and special. I believe there are times when we do hear a very strong voice, as in that incident on the Irish ferry, when God spoke so clearly to me, I was surprised that nobody else heard it. There will be times when we hear God's voice with that sort of quality. It may not be an audible sound, but it will come so strongly to you that it feels as if it has been spoken aloud.

Hearing God 'quietly'

When Jesus was led by the Spirit into the desert, as recorded in Luke chapter 4, and faced the temptations that the devil threw at Him, He did not hear an audible voice saying *'this is My Son, whom I love!'* But the scriptures came back into His memory. The Holy Spirit reminded Jesus of verses in the Old Testament which He used to counteract the devil's temptations. Jesus was hearing God, but in a different way. God was taking what was already in His mind and spirit and pulling it out and showing Him, 'that's how You are to answer the devil,' and Jesus spoke it out, *'it is written...* ' There are many times when God will speak like that to you. He will take a scripture, bring it up into your mind from deep within you and you know that it is the Word for that moment.

Timing

Listening to the Holy Spirit of God will affect the timing of the things that we do. There is the example in John chapter 7, when the Jewish Feast of Tabernacles was near. Everybody was expecting Jesus to go up there and His brothers said to Him, 'you ought to be going up to the feast. Isn't it about time to show Yourself?' and Jesus said 'no, I'm not going.' Then it says 'later He went' because He had the right timing from God.

There are many instances when we may know that we've got to go in a certain direction or do a certain thing but we're not actually sure of the timing. Well, we can go to God and say 'what's your timing on this?'

I remember we had a young woman living with us; she was in her mid-thirties, but at around the age of 16 she had become involved in a lot of addictive behaviour. God had set her free and now she was learning to come back into life. Despite her years she needed to grow in maturity. When people are taken into the grip of an addiction, their growth in maturity stops at that point, and the process does not recommence until they are freed from their bondage. Part of her growing up was to learn responsibility and to be trained in simple and ordinary things. She had never learnt to work, and making her work willingly was literally a hard task. She had a part-time job in the

Resources Centre of our ministry and as she also lived in our house, she had a responsibility to help me in the home as well.

I'm not particularly good at asking people to work for me. I'd rather do it myself, to be truly honest. It is not that I am unable to receive help, but I find it difficult to receive help from those who do it unwillingly. My response to that is, 'just move over, I'll do it myself.' Now she was meant to be helping me clean the house, and on this particular occasion which was Friday and I said to her 'could you vacuum the hall for me?' She vacuumed the hall, slammed the vacuum back where it belonged and went back upstairs to her bedroom. I pursued hot-foot after her and said 'please, can you come downstairs, and vacuum the lounge?'

Reluctantly she came downstairs, slumped round the lounge, pushed the vacuum cleaner in various directions and left it little different from when she had started. Then she was off to her bedroom again, and I could feel the anger rising in me. I was just about to move into my 'Rottweiler mode' when the Holy Spirit said, 'don't do anything rash, listen to me, I want to talk to you about this situation,' so I left what I was doing and went to my bedroom. I had actually spoken to Charles about this earlier as he was going off on a ministry trip for the weekend, and he had said 'she's your problem' so I went into my bedroom, knelt down and said 'Lord, speak to me. She's driving me mad.'

It did not take long before He began to tell me certain things which I wrote down; I then spoke to Him, 'Lord, if I say all this to her, she'll thump me.' She was quite capable of thumping me. He said 'you haven't asked me when you are to say these things to her,' so I said 'well, no I haven't. When do I say it to her?' His words were simple and clear, 'you say all this to her when she has apologised for the way she's been behaving.' I laughed and replied, 'you're funny, Lord, I've never heard her say she's sorry and I don't expect to hear it now.'

The Lord then said 'well, then you don't need to say anything to her.' It was as if a great burden had been lifted from me, because I had been ready for a real confrontation, but the Lord had said, in effect, 'no, just leave it. I've told you what to say, I've told you when to say it. Relax.' I thought 'wonderful' as I didn't have to get all my energy together to give this girl a strong rebuke. I just let it go and she went out of the house that evening.

The next morning when I got up, it was Saturday, the car she was driving had gone which made me somewhat anxious and I was thinking 'oh, Lord, she could do something stupid.' The Lord said 'just put her in My hands and leave it.' I spent the day doing something with the children and when we arrived back that evening she had laid the table and set in a log fire, which was quite unbelievable for her at that stage. She never normally did anything without being asked. As we all sat down to have tea and before I prayed a blessing over our food, she broke into the conversation and said 'I just want to say I'm sorry for the way I've been behaving.' Relief spread over the camp, and we all said 'oh, that's all right!'

It was then I felt the Lord say to me, 'now, you've got something to say to her.' I was squirming at that point because I still didn't want to say it, I didn't want to rock the boat. But obediently I added 'that's fine, you're forgiven, but after tea I need 10 minutes to talk with you. I need to tell you something.' Later I was able to say to her 'look, I know you were upset yesterday, I know you were in a mess, I know you were angry, so I prayed, and this is what the Lord told me to say to you, and I want to share it with you.'

There were some hard things to say, not just words to soothe and pacify, but she took it on the chin and received every one of them, because the timing was right. That's very important when listening to the Lord. You may know what He wants you to do, but get the timing right. Just say, 'When do I do it, Lord? Show me when.'

Inside information!

In John chapter 4, Jesus received knowledge and revelation from His Father. This story is well known – Jesus was at the well at Sychar, a woman came to Him and He engaged her in conversation. Very quickly He found His way right to the heart of the matter as He told her to *'go call your husband and come back.'* *'I have no husband'* she said, to which He replied *'you are right when you say you have no husband. The fact is, you have five husbands, and the man you now have is not your husband.'* He put His finger absolutely on the centre of the issue, though He had no knowledge of her other than what the Holy Spirit had given Him.

Once your ears have been opened to hear God, God has got a channel to impart to you the knowledge you need at any given time. This is why it's so exciting because when you are counselling people you haven't got to 'flail around' using all sorts of techniques to obtain answers. You only have to listen to the Lord.

'Lord, what's the matter with this person?' People will tell you all sorts with their mouth but the real problem, that deep need, the thing that is agonizing in them, that's what you've got to hear from the Lord, and only the Holy Spirit can give you that knowledge. As you train your ears to listen, when you are confronted with situations you cannot fathom, it is then that listening to the Lord will give you what you need.

As people with problems talk to me, I listen to them at one level with my natural ears, but beyond that I am reaching out desperately and saying, 'Lord, what are you saying? What are the needs of this person? What's in their heart?' I'm seeking to hear from the Spirit of God what the real problem is. Only God can see into the heart. He knows the hearts of men, but when you are in a situation when you've been given someone to help, then He will impart the knowledge that you need. It could come in a number of different forms.

Make my eyes to see

Do you remember when Jesus spent the night in prayer before He chose His disciples? Did He hear God say to Him 'one's going to be called Andrew, one's James, one's Matthew?' Did God speak, or did God show Him their faces? Have you ever thought about that? How did Jesus know who to pick? I have pondered upon that. Sometimes God speaks to us visually.

I only know a little of this and there is a great deal more that I have yet to explore; but very often before I come to a meeting or if I'm speaking or ministering I will say to the Lord, 'What do you want to do tonight?' and the Lord will show me. Sometimes He will show me particular faces and when I get into the meeting I'm almost looking for those people, because I know beforehand the Lord has shown me that they are the people for whom He has something very special. That releases my faith, because very often you will find that those are the people with very deep healing needs. They may have tremendous problems, but the fact that the Lord has shown them to you before you get there and you recognise their faces enables the Holy Spirit to release faith in you that He is going to do the miracle that He wants to do.

I have known Jean Darnall for many years and she has often been a guest in our home. If Jean is staying she will not eat before a meeting, and she doesn't want to talk to people; she just wants to get on her own. She has told me that many times the Lord shows her faces, just puts them before her and when she gets into the meeting she is aware of those to whom she needs to minister. She may not have all the knowledge she needs, but she knows where to begin.

I think it may well have happened when Jesus was picking the disciples, that as He waited on The Lord in prayer, God actually showed Him who they were. He certainly imparted to Him who He was to choose.

In John chapter 2:24 and 25 it says,

> *'But Jesus would not entrust himself to them, for He knew all men. He did not need man's testimony about man, for He knew what was in a man.'*

He knew them, He knows you, He knows me. He knows everything about us. As He looked at people

He saw faith, He saw unbelief, He saw demons, He saw grief and sadness, He read people's spirits. That's what God wants. He wants us to have eyes that see.

At the time when I was seeking the Lord to hear Him more clearly, God said to me 'we'll deal with your ears today.' The next week He said to me 'we'll deal with your eyes; do you want to see into the hearts of men?' then He said 'before you answer that question, I want to tell you that if you do, you'll not be able to neglect the things you see, so before you actually choose to see, you are going to have to understand that with it comes an awesome responsibility.' I said 'Lord, I do want to see.'

I had a neighbour who I found I could easily get irritated with. We had very little in common, and I am sure that she did not find me easy either, as we were so very different; but one day the Lord said to me 'look at her. Look at her with the eyes of the Spirit.' As I did, I began to see beyond the surface into the very needy heart beneath. I saw a person who was desperate for acceptance; insecure and needing so much love. Rather than rejecting her I felt a compassion for her and as I began to see into her heart I was able to pray, and to give to her. I was now not being put off by the signals that I received from the exterior but I was looking into the depths of that person's heart. I believe that is what God wants us all to do. We don't want merely to see each other on the surface, but we want to see the deep things in people's hearts. The Spirit of God will do that; seeing is part of perceiving. He knew their thoughts, Jesus saw right into the thoughts of men.

I can't say that it has happened to me very often, but it has on several occasions, I've been aware that people have been saying one thing with their mouths, but inside I can see that they are thinking something completely different.

And then you see Jesus didn't actually speak to what they said, He spoke to what they thought and he hit the target. In Matthew 9:4 it says that Jesus knew their thoughts. Now, we have the same Holy Spirit who gave Jesus this knowledge and understanding and He wants to give it to us.

Consider the Ananias and Sapphira incident in Acts chapter 5; what they said was plausible and sounded very generous – but it was not the truth which Peter, by the Holy Spirit, perceived. The consequences were dire. There are still charlatans about – those who set out to deceive; we need to be filled with the Holy Spirit and be discerning. We are warned about wolves among the sheep and as leaders need to be reading hearts by the Holy Spirit.

Chapter 6

Getting into the Action

I was the speaker at a ladies meeting in a church near Manchester, where a lady read a most wonderful poem which she had composed about Worry. It was hilariously funny, but there was no doubt that the Spirit of God had given it to her as it ministered forcefully to everybody. I talked to her about this gift of writing poetry and encouraged her to persist, and at the end of the weekend she came and gave me several poems, giving me permission to use them as I wanted to. I don't even know her name, she is one of God's precious sisters, Anonymous. I want to share one with you:

'Alone With God

I waited all day, but you never came.
I called to you gently, I called you by name.
Did you say to yourself "Well, He'll never miss
   me,
There's so many others He's eager to see.
What odds does it make, if I miss out a day?
I'll go to the meeting and there I can pray."
Yet, surely you know, I want you alone.

I called you and chose you to make you my
    own.
I've waited with longing to see your dear face.
There's no one else who can take your place.
The prayers that you pray, and your service, too
I'm glad that you know I'm working through
    you.
There are so many problems, you're praying
    them through.
The days are so busy, there's so much to do.
The family comes first, and you're tired of the
    pace
But I'm sad, because I've so missed seeing your
    face.
For a long time ago, way back in time,
I chose you, and named you and wanted you
    mine.
I thrilled as I formed you, I laughed at your
    birth
I joyed with my angels at the price of your
    worth.
Money can't buy you, you're more precious
    than gold
Kingdoms are nothing if you I can hold.
So here I will sit until you come to me
For I'm waiting and hoping that alone we can
    be.'

That's the heart of God to each one of us. He wants us to come aside and until we will take the time to organise ourselves, He's not going to speak. I think once we've become more experienced in hearing the voice of God, He can speak to us 'on the run'. But initially, in that training time He wants us to soak in

His presence, He wants us to hear Him. We've got to put in the work to get alone. And there are no short cuts to that.

I was reading a magazine article on Samson and Delilah and the question was 'What's the Delilah in your life?' Delilah robbed Samson of his anointing. And the question is 'what is it that robs you of your anointing?' And I had to answer in my heart 'busyness.' Simply being too busy to be quiet. Whenever I am quiet, whenever I seek the Lord, I hear the Lord, but often I miss out because I get too busy.

Even when we have been successful for a period of time we need to be on our guard, because there are times when life changes. Patterns of life go on for a short time, and then suddenly the dynamics of family life change. You have to readjust your programme, look at your day and say: 'what's the best time to be alone with God?' You have to make it, **you** have to make time, because remember it will never happen by itself; never. We all make time for the things that we love and the priorities that we create. You do what you want to do, basically. If you love gardening, you will find time to be in the garden. The house might look a mess, but the garden will look beautiful. Whatever you love, ultimately you will give yourself to. And God is speaking to you very strongly. He wants time with each one of you.

Focusing on God

Once you have set aside the time and found the place where you can be quiet and undisturbed, you can begin. I find that the first thing to do practically when I want to hear the Lord is to praise Him, because praise gets my focus and attention on God. It doesn't have to be long and extended, but I need to focus on the Lord. I usually take a few moments to be quiet and then say 'Lord, give me a song'; and I sing the first song that comes into my mind, because I believe the Holy Spirit will give me what I need at that moment to minister to my spirit.

Silencing the enemy

One of the reasons why praise is so important is because it silences the enemy. Psalm 8:2 says:

> *'From the lips of children and infants you have ordained praise because of your enemies, to silence the foe and the avenger.'*

I find that as I begin to use praise to quite deliberately focus on the Lord, it silences the voice of the enemy.

At the moment we start the adventure of hearing God, probably our greatest fear is that we may hear the wrong voice. This can easily stop us from listening at all. Because we don't want to be considered wacky, we don't want to hear crazy things, so perhaps we don't even listen at all. Consequently, it is important to understand that praise silences the voice of the enemy more effectively than anything else, because the devil is allergic to praise. I don't think we've even begun to explore the extent which the enemy hates the praises of God. I think if we knew his hatred of the worship of God, we would use it more.

I was reading a book recently about the Chinese church and the way that they use praise in the most impossible situations and how God performed the same miracles for them as He did in the New Testament. The book told of two 19-year-old girls who had been beaten, and terribly abused, one of whom had broken ribs. They had been manacled inside a prison in China and they were starving. But as they were in that prison cell they began to praise God, on and on they went, raising more and more praises to the living, powerful God, and as they praised Him the chains physically fell off. That is a true story which only proves the point I have been making. Praise is one of the weapons we need to learn to use more effectively. It is a spiritual weapon that God has put in our hands which silences the enemy.

Filtering out 'you'

Because you have set your heart to listen to the Lord, because you've decided to praise Him and you're coming to listen to Him, His desire is to speak to you and He's going to speak in a way that you can recognise, so don't be afraid of the bit that's you. Because you'll recognise that it's you. You'll look back later on and you'll say, 'well, I know that part was the Lord, but I think that bit was probably me.' But it doesn't really matter, because you're on a training programme and it will get clearer as you go on.

As I said in an earlier chapter, listening to the voice of the Lord is like being a musician whose ear is trained to hear one particular instrument. You can always pick out the instrument that you're familiar with. And the more time you spend listening to the Lord, the more you will tune out your extraneous thoughts and tune in God.

Part of this tuning-in process involves recognising

where we receive the voice of God. Do you hear him in your mind? No, receiving from God goes on in a much deeper part of you. It is in your guts, some would call it your belly; it is in fact your innermost being.

I find it helps some people when I ask them, 'where in you, is the voice of conscience?' When you know you've done something wrong and you feel guilty, where do you hear the guilt and shame? Where is that intuitive, sensitive part of you that is your conscience? You will hear the voice of God in the same place. It's deep within you. It's a part of you which in most of us is very undeveloped. That is where you hear.

It is important to understand that those things that you hear from God are not necessarily perfect, or else we would be tempted to add them to the back of our Bibles. There will always be a mixture in what you hear. It will be a mixture of the flesh and of the Spirit, your natural thoughts and the thoughts of God. If you read the books of the Old Testament prophets, particularly the minor prophets, you get the voice of God very clearly. And we believe that all Scripture is God breathed. But you hear something of the personality of the prophets, of the men, as you read. So, something of what you hear will definitely be the Spirit of God, but somehow it will have something of you in it as well. And hopefully the more sensitive you become to God, the more it will be of His Spirit and less of you. In the early stages I believe there will definitely be a bit of a mixture.

There are times that you will hear the bones of the thing God is wishing to communicate without perfectly having all the details. There is the example of a prophet in the New Testament called Agabus, which is recorded in Acts 21:10–14. Paul is staying in the house of Philip the Evangelist who has four married daughters who prophesy. It states,

> *'After we had been there for a number of days, a prophet named Agabus came down from Judea. Coming over to us, he took Paul's belt, tied his own hands and feet with it and said "The Holy Spirit says, 'In this way the Jews of Jerusalem will bind the owner of this belt and will hand him over to the Gentiles.'" When we heard this, we and the people there pleaded with Paul not to go up to Jerusalem. Then Paul answered "Why are you weeping and breaking my heart? I am ready not only to be bound, but also to die in Jerusalem for the name of the Lord Jesus." When he would not be dissuaded we gave up and said "The Lord's will be done."'*

It was important that the prophetic word was given. Undoubtedly the prophet had heard the Lord, but so had Paul. Whenever you are bringing a word which you have heard from God to give to someone else and it is directional, your responsibility is to give what you have heard. The responsibility of the person who hears it is to discern whether it is the Lord's word for them or not. I do not believe that we are to impose what we hear on anybody else. It's dangerous. But when somebody actually brings something and says 'I believe the Lord has said this to me for you' then you have to listen to the voice of the Spirit of God in you and when that creates uncertainty in your own spirit, you have to take it and say 'thank you', but go back to the Lord with it. It is only when you have the confirmation in your own spirit that you can be sure it is a word from the Lord. Paul is obviously doing that internal double-check here. He didn't reject it, but he didn't receive it, or at least not in the way the others received it. It did not prevent him from going to Jerusalem. That's important, very important. There are a lot of odd cases around, where people are living on a prophetic word which someone gave them 20 years ago, and they are ineffective in ministry because they are waiting for the word to be fulfilled. We've all experienced cases of that. The prophetic word from God is simply a confirmation of what you're already hearing from the Lord.

When you go to the end of the story, we find that when Paul arrived in Jerusalem, the Jews stirred up trouble and the Roman Commander came up, arrested him and ordered him to be bound with two chains.

Now go back to the prophetic word. You will notice that Agabus hadn't got the details right, but he had got the general sense right. He said that 'the Jews are going to bind you.' They didn't, the Romans did. The prophetic word was bringing a warning that trouble was ahead and that Paul was going to be bound. I think Paul already knew that, by his response to the prophecy, and was prepared for it. I want you to see that there is a mixture, part is from the Spirit of God, yet there is something of the human too which means the prophecy was not totally accurate. And the emotional reaction of the outsiders to the message initially stopped them understanding, and might have put Paul off if he'd let it.

And yet, the scripture says quite clearly that Agabus was a prophet. I think it's important because sometimes we think if we don't get it absolutely correct we're no good. But that's not what the New Testament says. They accepted him and received him as hearing the prophetic word of God, even though the details were not absolutely perfect. I'm encouraged by that scripture because we don't always dot every 'i' and cross every 't', but we're seeking to hear God and get the general sense.

This is also confirmed in 1 Corinthians 13:9, which says,

> *'For we know in part and we prophesy in part, but when perfection comes the imperfect disappears.'*

Chapter 7

Encouragement, Correction, Instruction

What specific things do we hear from God, as we listen to Him on a daily basis? This chapter will begin to answer this question. However, you will need to use your notebook if you are seriously wanting to hear God's daily communication for your own situation. Before He ever gets around to giving you words for others or for the Church, God wants to speak to you personally. If you want answers, you need to ask questions. I suggest that you write down in the front of your notebook the three key questions that are being dealt with in this chapter. These are the questions that I personally ask the Lord each day, and you will find they will help you to get started.

Have You got a word of encouragement for me?

This is the first question I ask the Lord. I need to be encouraged. After asking the question, I am simply quiet and I listen. We can be confident that encouragement will be given, because the character of prophecy is that it will encourage, strengthen and comfort (1 Corinthians 14:3). That's what Scripture says. So whatever I'm truly hearing from God will have those elements in it. I want the Lord, by the Spirit of God, to encourage me, and He always does.

Sometimes we are afraid to listen to God because we believe that the first thing he will bring to us is a rebuke for all the ways we have failed and grieved Him. But that is not how a loving father speaks to his child. Think of how you treat your own children when they come to you and look at you with those wide enquiring eyes. 'Have I done it right?' You know, even if they have done part of it wrong, and you need to tell them that as well, you'll tell them first of all, 'yes, you were great, that was really great, but ... ' I hope you do that. Because we all need reassurance, love and affirmation, don't we?

We all have a basic need to be encouraged, and we need to encourage each other. Even when we've got to correct one another, let's encourage, let's build up. As British people we're not very good at it. Americans are wonderful. If you've ever been to the States or lived there, you'll know they are great encouragers, it's one of their strengths, they will always say something positive to you. We British have the tendency to always be negative. But God is always positive.

Do you need to correct me?

This is my next question to the Lord, after I have received His words of love and encouragement. 'Is there something I'm doing that You're not happy with? Because I do want to please you, Lord.'

Ephesians 5:10 says,

> *'Find out what pleases the Lord.'*

Paul in writing to Timothy says,

> *'All Scripture is God breathed and is useful for teaching, rebuking, correcting and training in righteousness.'* (2 Timothy 3:16)

I therefore want the Holy Spirit to tell me if I'm doing something that doesn't please Him. When we are open to the Lord, He'll tell us quite quickly. He may use a verse of Scripture or He may speak directly. What I've discovered is that He doesn't heap a whole pile of guilt and condemnation on me, but deals with me gently yet strongly. Also, He deals with me in a way which always gives me a doorway of forgiveness and a way to change. That's the difference between dealings with the devil and with the Lord. The devil always heaps failure and condemnation on you and makes you feel it's impossible to change.

When God is correcting you, He shows you the problem, but always gives you the way out, and the choice as to whether you want to escape. He will be persistent, if you are serious; He will prod you until you do something about it. I've usually found that if I've asked God to show me something, yet don't deal with it, He won't take me on to anything else, He goes back and back again. He's better than a terrier dog with a rabbit. And He will not show you very much more until you deal with the thing you've asked Him to bring into the light.

David said,

> *'Create in me a pure heart, O God, and renew a steadfast spirit within me.'* (Psalm 51:10)

Psalm 24 tells us it's the one who has clean hands and a pure heart, who hasn't lifted up his soul to an idol or sworn by what is false, who is going to ascend the hill of the Lord. So, it's a priority to God that we should be pure, and He is very good at shining His light as you open up to Him. He will show you clearly and simply, He doesn't make heavy weather of it.

God also speaks to us through dreams. Job 33:14–18 says,

> *'For God does speak – now one way, now another – though man may not perceive it. In a dream, in a vision of the night, when deep sleep falls on men as they slumber in their beds, he may speak in their ears and terrify them with warnings, to turn man from wrongdoing and keep him from pride, to preserve his soul from the pit, his life from perishing by the sword.'*

This is an area that I'm learning about at the moment. I've never really taken an awful lot of notice of dreams, but if you look through the Old Testament, on many occasions God used dreams to speak His Word to people. It continues in the New Testament, Joseph was warned by angels in a dream, the wise men did not return to Herod because of what was revealed in a dream. Ask the Holy Spirit to use your dreams to impress upon you things that you ought to be listening to more carefully. Our dreams may be caused merely by too much food too late at night, and that's just human. But there are times when, in actual fact, it's the Spirit of God wanting to speak to us.

I woke up one night during an early Eagle Camp, and I'd had a bizarre dream. The details are not important, they were rather crazy, but essentially I woke up feeling guilty because in this dream I'd told a half-truth. The dream was quite clear, I knew that I'd told it, I knew what I'd said. I knew it wasn't the truth and I knew I'd been found out and I woke up feeling guilty.

I asked the Lord, 'what are You saying?' He just said to me, 'I want to deal with this character trait where you know you are capable of telling half-truths, because there are times when you do what you thought was horrific in your dream and don't even notice it.' The following night I was sitting in the Camp meeting, and the Lord said to me 'ask Me for a coal off the altar to purify your lips. Let me deal with that. I gave it to you in a dream so that the real sense of horror could come over to you, then you could see yourself and what you had done. Even though you hadn't done it, you knew potentially you were quite capable of doing it. Now let me deal with it and root it out of you.' I was very thankful to the Lord for that.

I can't give you many examples because I've not been listening to dreams very long, but I think that Scripture is quite clear that God wants to speak through dreams.

Are there any specific instructions for me?

We have this promise from the Psalms,

> *'I will instruct you and teach you in the way you should go; I will counsel you and watch over you.'*
>
> (Psalm 32:8)

So this is usually quite an interesting question because very often I've made my own plans, and the Lord knows that. He does know that you've got a job of work to do, He knows if you have a family to care for. There are certain basics that need to be done simply to keep life going. God knows that. But beyond that, 'Lord, what is your agenda for to-day?' It amazes me how direct God will be, if I give Him the opportunity.

Sometimes He will flash somebody's face into my mind, or He'll remind me of someone's need. I then go back to Him with it and ask 'are you telling me to do "such and such"?' and wait to hear a 'yes' or a 'no'. His voice may be gently saying 'try and fit it in – they need you.' Sometimes I'll go back and say 'but Lord, I've go to do this, this and this' and He'll say 'when you have done those pressing tasks you will still have time to do what I have told you.' Sometimes I'm all set for a busy day that I have planned myself, but say 'Lord, I want to do what you want me to do to-day' and a number of times God has surprised me by saying 'do nothing, I want you to relax to-day.'

Once God said to me 'do something you want to do, enjoy yourself.' I was thinking 'oh, I can't do that.' He said 'no, no, no, you need to relax, you need to unwind, need to please yourself to-day. Do something you enjoy doing.' Now when God has told you to do it, you don't feel guilty. But so often we are so work-orientated that we feel guilty when we're not actually doing something we can justify as good honest work. That's why we need to hear the Lord.

Sometimes we have emotions and feelings that we cannot understand or explain to ourselves. I've always found it's good to ask the Lord. 'Lord, why am I feeling like this? What's up with me? Why am I feeling so heavy, Lord? What's going on inside me? Why am I reacting like this?' He will tell you. I don't know exactly how He'll tell you, but He will. He does it for me, and He won't treat you any differently.

I know, too, that when you're listening to the Lord, He will use your questioning to speak to you and warn you of dangers. I woke up one morning, whether I'd been dreaming or not I don't know because I couldn't remember having a dream. But as I came to consciousness I was disturbed, I felt heavy, I felt fearful. As I don't usually wake up like that I said 'Lord, have I had a bad dream? What am I feeling?' It wasn't just something I was able to throw off after having a shower and by saying to myself, 'come on, wake up, get on with the day.' It was a heavy feeling inside of me. And I said, 'Lord, what is it that I am sensing?' Immediately (it may well be that I had dreamed it), a picture flashed through my mind. I knew that I was planning to take a friend who was staying with us down to Wells, which is a lovely city fairly nearby. I always take a route which goes over the top of the Mendip Hills. I know the road very well, but at that moment the Lord flashed into my mind the picture of a bad bend. Now, I knew it was a bad bend, I'd been on the road lots of times. I felt the Lord say to me 'cover the journey in prayer.' So I prayed and said, 'Lord, I don't really know what's going on here, but I'm just praying and I'm asking you to protect us. We're planning to go to Wells, is it right that we go?' I felt the assurance to carry on, but I felt the Holy Spirit pressing upon me, to protect the journey.

It is very easy to forget these things as you get into the activity of the day. It was not until I was driving towards Wells in the car that I suddenly remembered. 'Now, yes, what was that funny thing that happened to me this morning?' As it came back into my memory I checked my speed and was ready for the bad bend. Suddenly there was an enormous lorry in the middle of the road. Had I been there two seconds earlier I may not have survived crashing into it. In fact a tree had come down blocking half the carriageway, and the lorry had taken evasive action and was filling my side of the road. Had I not been warned in my spirit, I'd have probably bombed round that corner at my normal speed.

I'm so glad I asked the Lord what was going on in my spirit that morning. I know that it is important that you train yourself to ask the Lord what it is you're reacting to, before you suffer the consequences. Sometimes you don't know what it is, you simply feel very heavy. It could possibly be lack of sleep, or some other very practical thing. But it may be that the Spirit of God is trying to give you a warning. Learn to ask those sort of questions.

As we become more experienced, we will learn to hear the voice of God 'on the run'. I remember an incident when one of Colin Urquhart's daughters, about 15 or 16 years old, was Christmas shopping in London. She had been trained in the family to be sensitive to the voice of the Lord. Suddenly the Spirit of God said to her 'get out of this shop.' She immediately said to her friend 'we're going, we've got to get out of here, God's told me to get out of here.' The friend was more than a little perplexed. (I don't know whether she was a believer.) It was only about 4.30 in the afternoon but Claire knew she had to get out of the shop urgently. Half an hour later the IRA bomb went off in Harrods.

This is a serious business and I'm not joking when I say it can be a matter of life and death. If we have an ear for the voice of God, the Holy Spirit can warn us when there is imminent danger.

I have given you three basic questions that you can use daily, but as you continue you will discover that you can ask the Lord anything. It is good to begin simply as it gives the Lord the opportunity to start speaking to you. Let me remind you again, you need to be warned that once you embark upon this adventure the enemy will tell you that you're making it up. Do not let him deceive you, believe the opposite. He's a liar, his native language is lies. He doesn't want you to hear the voice of God, so he'll tell you that you can't hear or he'll tell you it's rubbish. Or else he'll slip something in to mislead you: so **weigh** things once you've written them down. But persevere. And you'll find even a week after you've started and look back to the first day; as you read what you have written in your notebook you'll say 'it was You, Lord, Thank **You**.'

A few practical cautions

1. Words that stimulate anxiety or fear are not from God. Fear is a tool of the enemy. Philippians 4:6 says *'Do not be anxious about anything'* so it is unlikely that

God will be making you anxious – He may be seeking to warn you, as in the road to Wells incident. Proverbs 1:33:

> *'Whoever listens to me will live in safety and be at ease, without fear of harm.'*

A friend of mine was listening to God for each of her children one day – very shortly after she'd first discovered she could listen – and she thought she heard Him say, '... she will need you by the end.' She was left with a horrible feeling that something ghastly was going to happen to her daughter (terminal disease? early death?). Needless to say she was very upset. Her husband asked the Lord about it and received a reassuring answer. She managed to put the experience behind her, but it was only over time that she realised that what she'd heard was the devil trying to put fear into her and maybe create an opening for some future plan of his own. So if you hear something that knocks you sideways like that, **always** double check with the Lord and other people. **God's** warnings are **always** constructive and lead to good.

2. Our own desires can influence what we are hearing, especially when emotions are involved. Strong-willed or ardent people particularly need to watch this. It is difficult, but possible, to lay our desires aside – Galatians 2:20:

> *'I have been crucified with Christ and I no longer live, but Christ lives in me!'*

I remind myself of that scripture, offer my will, emotions, thoughts, desires to God again and say

'I don't want my way but Yours, and so in Jesus' Name I bind every fleshly desire in this situation. I don't want to be deceived, I want to hear You, Lord.' If I ask my father for bread will He give me a stone instead? No. Matthew 7:7–11 says,

> *'the Father in heaven will give good gifts to those who ask Him.'*

Sometimes our lives are dominated by unfulfilled desires – maybe for a partner or a child. God desires us to live in peace, to set our affection on things above and to seek first the Kingdom of God and His righteousness. Then He promises all things will be added to us. We can't order or demand from God so let Him care for these sensitive areas of need.

I heard Larry Christenson tell of an incident from his family which illustrates this. He was due for a sabbatical and had chosen to spend it in the mid-west of the USA near his parents. At this time they were living in California, his eldest son was at college and did not want to move. Wills clashed and it seemed an impossible deadlock. God spoke and asked both of them if they would lay down their will in this situation and expect that He would answer with His. It's never easy to back down, it's humbling and painful – you feel very vulnerable. But they were obedient and very quickly God spoke through a younger daughter. Why doesn't 'X' spend one semester in California, one with family mid-west and finish his year back in California? Why not, indeed? It was agreed, peace was restored, and as it happened he met his future wife in the mid-west and discovered yet again 'God's ways are higher than our ways!'

3. Be careful about specifics – times, dates, etc. The devil loves to make you give up. He knows we love things clear-cut and specific, so he leads us to magnify small things and get convinced about unnecessary specifics – which taken overall don't matter; but if they are not fulfilled it can easily knock our confidence, make us feel foolish and never try again to hear God. I have known people convinced that they will have specifically a son or a daughter and they are sure God told them so. He is quite able to do that, we have scriptural evidence; but I find myself saying: Do you **need** to know? And if you've got it wrong, so what? You're wearing 'L' plates aren't you? It's all part of learning. Try again, but don't give up. The disciples made mistakes, learned through them, went on and got it right. We are no different.

4. Ask for specific information after receiving general instructions. A friend heard the Lord say, 'I want to heal my people and teach you faith. Pray against moles on people's skin.' She was reminded of this when standing behind a man in the supermarket checkout. He had a large and ugly mole on his neck. She prayed inwardly in obedience and saw nothing happen. Immediately came the thought 'you made that up. If God had spoken then it should have vanished.' It really shook her confidence. Later she asked the Lord what had gone wrong. He answered 'I do want you to pray against moles, but not for every mole you see – just for those that are not harmless.' Some little time later she was in a prayer meeting and two friends voiced the fact they both had moles causing problems. She was put on the spot and she had to pray for them, since there was no one else there. Her faith level was zero! Later she was astonished but glad to hear that one mole disappeared and the other stopped being a nuisance.

Another time her teenage daughter was suffering verbal abuse and unpleasant behaviour from school friends because of her Christian witness. Whilst praying into the situation, she heard the words 'get up and fight, both of you.' She knew this might be her natural reaction and not the Lord, so she asked Him if this was His instruction, to say it again in words she wouldn't use, so she could be sure she was hearing Him. He responded 'pick up the anvil and hit the enemy with it!' In other words, the devil in the kids was striking at the Lord in her daughter – so the Lord's power had to be directed at the devil, rather than anyone wasting energy in fighting on human terms.

5. Don't be afraid to admit failure and don't let mistakes rob you. It is always our pride that is hurt and God wants that dealt with anyway, so press on. God never gives up.

Chapter 8

The Three-Monthly Check Up – the Family

About every three months or so, I try to have an extended time of listening to God when I can ask Him wider questions. I have found this to be very, very useful, particularly concerning family life.

I begin by saying, 'Lord, will you speak to me about the children?' And I take each child in our family and their partners now, because four of them are married, and I say 'Lord, talk to me, tell me what I need to know at this point in their lives so that I can pray effectively for them.' As parents we're aware of the strengths and weaknesses of our own families, we're aware of areas of difficulty. You have a choice: ignore it, worry about it, or seek the Lord and hear what He has to say and put your faith behind what He says, and use it to bring focus to your prayers. If you do not bother to ask, the chances are you simply become enslaved to worry.

I've found constantly that the Lord will talk to me when I ask him direct questions. He'll show me something quite specific. He'll actually say to me 'target on that, pray for it. That needs to happen in this one's life, pray for it.' I started on this some years ago. Colin was about to go on a ministry trip abroad, and I had asked him if he would go and see my sister and take some things to her, as she lived near to where he would be ministering. He had agreed to do this. My sister did not have a living faith in Jesus, and I hoped that this contact would help in bringing her nearer to the Lord. I was taken by surprise when he turned and said to me 'What's the Lord saying to you about your sister?' I had no answer, and felt like a grasshopper looking for a hole in which to hide – the reason being that I had not thought of asking the Lord anything, and consequently the Lord had said nothing to me. My constant prayer had simply been, 'Lord, please save her.'

Now I was confronted with this question, 'have you asked the Lord to talk to you about your sister?' to which I had replied, 'no, I haven't.' His response was, 'well, do.' I knew him well enough to know that he would come back to me to find out what I had heard. So I went to the Lord and asked Him to speak to me about my sister. And He did. He quite clearly gave me three specific things that were binding her. I had not drawn them out of my conscious thinking, because they were descriptions that I wouldn't naturally have used of my sister. Even as I heard them from the Spirit of God, I readily recognised them to be the truth. I was so thrilled by the revelation I had received that I remember rushing downstairs, grabbing hold of Charles and saying 'this is what the Lord's said to me.' In my excitement I just cried out, 'set her free, Lord, set her free from these things.' But the Lord said 'no, what you bind on earth will be bound in heaven, what you loose on earth will be loosed in heaven.' Jesus had taught this to his disciples, as recorded in Matthew 16:19. He clearly said to me 'now take authority, because I've given you authority: bind and loose.' I began to pray for my sister totally differently from the way I had at any time in my life.

This taught me to be specific and ask questions about how I should be praying for my children. Find out how you should be praying for your children. What are your faith goals for them? God always honours faith. What's your faith picture for each one of your children? How do you want to see them? Then hold on to it.

Our eldest boy Craig was a rebel, a real rebel. I come from a family of them, it's a family trait from which we have needed to be set free, because there was a kind of in-built dicky-oppositeness in all of us. At 13 we despaired of Craig ever following the Lord. Everything was 'boring'. We were perhaps at that time in one of the best ministry centres in the country, but everybody was boring, it didn't matter who it was. And I remember saying to him 'is God boring?' and he said 'no, God's all right, it's just the rest of you Christians.' You get the truth from 13-year-olds!

As I began to pray, God gave me a picture of using Craig's strength and his 'Joe Blunt' black and white personality in the Kingdom of God, rather than in the other kingdom. His name, Craig, means rock-like, and I began to pray 'Lord, make him into a rock, make him solid, make him into a rock in Your Kingdom.' Whenever I saw contrary evidence I would reject it, close my eyes and see what God had said, and make that the focus of my prayer.

Things got worse before they got better. God gave me a promise from Isaiah 44:3 for Craig and my other children. I had a choice – believe what God said and exercise faith in seeing the result of faith – His Spirit and blessing poured out on Craig; or allow images derived from fear to dominate my imagination. I chose to believe. God began to capture Craig's heart and turn his strength God-ward. To-day he is still very black and white but full of God's word and that strength helps others to stand firm.

About that time I remember reading a book by Catherine Marshall who had done something similar. She had cut out pieces of paper in the shape of an egg and had written Bible verses on them; promises about what God had said to her about each of her children and she had placed them within the pages of her Bible and prayed over them saying, 'these are eggs which I expect to hatch.' Years later she testified how she had almost forgotten about them, but when she discovered them and pulled them out she found that God had been faithful to His promises, because He's faithful to all that He has promised.

I would encourage you to do that on behalf of your children. Other questions I use are, 'what plans do you have for my children? Speak to me, Lord. What promises do you have for them?'

When you're battling in family relationships, and particularly with strong-willed children, it is very easy to clash. There were times in our home when we were battling with the wills of our children, particularly in the teenage years. I remember one day having a particularly difficult verbal battle with one of my daughters. I knew it was wrong, I knew I'd got into anger and strife. We were going hammer and tongs at each other. Once she had gone off to school and I settled down to be quiet and listen, the Holy Spirit spoke to me and said 'you're battling against the wrong thing' which caused me to stop and say, 'OK, Lord, what should I be battling against?'

God said to me 'the spirit of the age that's operating in her is what you need to be attacking, not your daughter.' My response to this was, 'OK, Lord, what is the spirit of the age?' His reply was, 'it's the spirit that's at work in the schools, it's a spirit of rebellion, it's a spirit of anti-authority and it is gripping the hearts of most young people in this generation. It's come into your home and you haven't recognised it, and you're fighting with her. You are aware of the fact that she's being awkward and she's a teenager, but you actually need to be fighting with the deeper thing which is the spirit of the age, which is operating in her, the spirit of rebellion.'

Once I'd heard that from God I knew I had something to do and I took authority over that spirit power, I forbade it to come over my doorstep. I even opened the front door and prayed out and said 'if you're in the school, and you get on my daughter, you will drop off her the moment she comes through this door. You're not coming in this house.' In fact, I told the enemy he wasn't coming on my daughter either, and began to pray accordingly. I can tell you, within about three days we saw a total change in her behaviour – it was remarkable. I learned a big lesson because I saw the evidence before my own eyes; and it had come almost immediately.

If you find yourself in a similar battle, and you win the victory but later on stop praying, you may well see the problem re-emerging and then you need to enter the battle again, because you must be vigilant. You will know what to pray for, because the enemy's tactics are very predictable, once you've discovered what they are and the way he's working. But you need to listen so that you will know what to do.

There are times, as I've said before, when you are listening to the Lord, and He will show you things in picture form. Be open to that, because it's still the voice of the Lord. Some people are much more responsive to pictures than words. I'm not really a television person; I'm not a video person. I don't receive very much through the visual. I'd much rather have the radio on and be doing something at the same time. Now that's my nature at a human level and it seems that God speaks to me in words rather than visually, although at times He does give me pictures and images. But some people more readily see the visual.

When King David had committed adultery with Bathsheba, God spoke to Nathan the prophet and showed him a life situation in picture form which he described in words to David. Nathan didn't go directly to David and say 'God's told me you've committed adultery.' He may well have lost his head in the process or he could have easily chopped off David's ears by that blunt approach. No, he simply described the picture the Lord had given him; David's response enabled him to speak the word of God and gain immediate repentance.

Be open for that, particularly with your children. It's easier to say 'I was praying for you, and God showed me a picture,' and describe the picture to them and let the Spirit of God interpret it to them. Because if you simply say it in words, it may well sound like criticism, and you won't be heard.

What the Lord shows us about our children may well need dealing with in a very practical way. I remember at one time one of our sons, who was in his late teens, was quite emotionally involved with a young woman who we perceived was manipulating him. That's always bad news, particularly in a male/female relationship. I could see this and knew I needed to speak to him about it. I also knew that I could not choose just any time because whenever I made any comment about this relationship he closed his ears. So I asked the Lord how I was to handle what He had shown me, and He gave me a scripture. He said to me, 'tell him to guard his heart, it is the well-spring of life' from Proverbs 4:23, and I said 'OK, Lord, I'll tell him that but please give me the right opportunity.'

About two weeks later he came and sat on the end of our bed and said 'Mum, will you take this splinter out, I can't get to it.' I took the splinter out and as he was just sitting there chatting with me and we were in harmony, talking about all sorts of ordinary things, I felt the prompting of the Holy Spirit and then I said to him 'you know, I was praying for you the other night and the Lord gave me a scripture for you.' I gave him the scripture without adding any comment. He began to open up and then I was able to say a few things, just warnings, but God was able to take that and use it.

Sometimes we say too much. But if our children are the Lord's then let's allow the Spirit of God to do the disciplining because He knows each one of them. But we've got to put the word in. Sometimes you have to confront situations, just as Nathan knew he had to confront David. Ask the Lord for His wisdom to know how to do it, He'll give it to you.

Chapter 9

The Three-Monthly Check Up –
Finding God's Priorities

We're living in a world where people have expectations which they want you to fulfil, particularly when you have Christian leadership responsibility. Many would love us to be puppets on which they could pull the strings, and make us do what they want us to do. Sometimes these actions are unintentional, but that is the effect they have.

The only solution is to know what God wants you to do and then you can say 'no' to the other things. But if you haven't first asked what you should be doing, I can almost guarantee that you won't say 'no' to things that you should not be doing.

'What plans do you have for me?'

Life is always changing, and we need to review it. I can remember a particular time when all the children were at school; they were fairly young and I had been doing a lot of speaking at women's meetings which I enjoyed. One particular time when I had accepted one of these invitations, I'd rushed out, taken the afternoon women's meeting, but come back in to find the house in chaos, no tea ready and everybody putting me under pressure. Other members of our household had also been busy that afternoon, and there were more activities that evening. Consequently, by the end of the day I was absolutely frazzled. Yet when people invited me, and it seemed I had the time to do what they wanted, I didn't know how to say 'no'.

I had to go back to the Lord and say 'do You want me to be taking these meetings?' The Lord gave me the answer I needed, but also addressed a much wider issue in my life. He asked me a key question, 'what do you think is My main calling on your life at this moment?' The answer at that time was that I needed to provide a home that was peaceful for Charles, who was at the sharp end of ministry. I needed to provide a home for my children, where they had a 'mum' who had quality time for them. I needed to create a place where there was order, because you can't work peacefully out of chaos. It disturbs your spirit if there is always a backlog of work, and you're not on top of things.

I also had three single people, who were part of the Bethany Fellowship, living in our house as extended family. I knew there were many times when they were irritated with me because I couldn't give them any quality time. It seemed that my only communication time with them was 'on the run', or when the kids were finished with. And on a couple of occasions they would say things like 'can't we just go out and have a meal together? Can't we go to the cinema?' And I kept putting them off.

The Lord said to me 'they need you too, at this moment in your life they are part of your list of priorities. I'm your number one priority, you need to worship me and have time for me, but your number two priority is that you need to have a home where there is peace. After you've established that peace and you're fulfilling the needs of all these people who are your immediate responsibility, if somebody then asks you to do something else, and you are able do it and can say "yes, I can do it and I'd enjoy doing it"; then do it. But stop saying "yes" when you should be saying "no".'

Now, you can relate that to your own circumstances; mine have changed since that time, I now have different priorities. But you need to know what you should be doing, and the only way you'll get to know is by listening to God.

I have already said that the thing that potentially robs me of my anointing is busyness. So this is a message I have constantly to preach to myself. I could fill every moment of every day with people on the end of the telephone asking 'will you? Will you? Will you?' I don't find it easy to say 'no'. My natural instinct would be to say 'yes', but I am learning to say 'no' because I've first heard what God wants me to do. It's essential, particularly for those of you in a leadership capacity, that you know what God wants you to do, because otherwise you're just running round like a chicken with its head chopped off. And you will not be able to hear the Lord.

This is a developing thing, it is an adventure. Learn to trust the Spirit of God within you. Job 32:8 and 9 says,

> *'But it is the Spirit in a man, the breath of the Almighty, that gives him understanding. It is not*

> *only the old who are wise, not only the aged who understand what is right.'*

And you have the Spirit of God in you, and the breath of the Almighty gives you understanding. It is part of hearing God.

Many years ago I met Arthur Wallis, and over the years had the privilege of getting to know him quite well. Arthur used to stay in our home from time to time. We were very new in the things of the Spirit, so it was so good to have a father in God, who you could ask those burning questions that constantly arose. I would ask him 'how do you hear God?' and, 'how do you hear this?' and, 'what about this, and what about that?' He was very patient with me. I remember one day asking him 'what's your ministry?' He looked quite sad as he answered and said, 'my ministry is that of a prophet, God has appointed me a prophet.' He continued, 'even as I am telling you, I feel very sad, because I'm not giving God enough time to speak.'

He was in fact a good writer, a good communicator, a good public speaker, and he had been pressurised into roles. Perhaps because he was living trusting the Lord for his income it was almost a case of, 'if you don't do meetings and you don't perform, are you going to get enough money to feed the family?' This is a pressure for many people in ministry. He had actually neglected the time that was needed to be spent in the presence of God to hear the voice of God. And he said it to me with great sadness.

I believe that in the years that followed, because I'm talking of many years ago now, he moved into a situation where there was more support and he had more ability to spend time listening to God.

But I always remember it as a warning. Because if you're going to develop the whole prophetic gifting which essentially is what I'm teaching in this book, then you're going to have to spend time with God. And if you already know how to hear God, don't let the enemy rob you and rob the Body of Christ of that gifting. It's such a precious gifting, but it needs time, and it needs quiet. And only you can provide God with that time.

Chapter 10

Eagerly Desire Spiritual Gifts

As you develop your ability to hear the voice of God, and you become confident that the Holy Spirit is speaking to you, this becomes the doorway to the spiritual gifts, the hearing gifts of the Spirit, the prophetic, the words of knowledge, words of wisdom, discerning of spirits.

It all comes through the same channel. The development of this training, which opens your ears to the Lord, will move you into the gift of prophecy. Let me give you a definition of prophecy which I have found very helpful:

> 'Prophecy expresses the heart of God, through the words of a man, into a person or a group, in any situation, for the purpose of building up in faith and love.'

As you have followed the message of this book you have been learning how to open your ears, listen to the Lord, and speak out or write down what He gives. Up to now we've dealt with it on a personal level, but the gift of prophecy is to be used in the Church. It can in fact be used in any situation, but essentially in this chapter and the next I'm talking about bringing that gift into the corporate gathering, whether that's house-group or Church.

I want to be very practical, both about the dangers and abuses, as well as the positive side. There are two big dangers with prophecy – either we do not speak because of fear of getting it wrong and making a mess of it, or we go to the other extreme and we bring so much that it's difficult to pick out that which is really the voice of God and what is just fleshly. I want to talk about these two danger zones.

I know a lot of people, when they start to listen to God, are anxious not to make mistakes. How can we test what we're hearing and see if it's God or the flesh?

Does it honour Jesus?

Ask yourself how Jesus would react if He were listening to these words. Is this prophecy in harmony with the teachings of the Gospels? Is this word bringing glory to the Name of Jesus?

Does it agree with Scripture?

The voice of the Spirit will always speak in accordance with the Word of God. Someone came to me the other day saying, 'I've had a prophetic word about my situation, God's told me that this relationship is perfectly all right, it's got His stamp of approval on it.' Now it's not easy to say to somebody 'that's not the voice of God.' But if that person is involved in an adulterous relationship and telling you 'it's OK, God says it's all right,' you have to. We need to stand our ground and say 'I'm sorry, that's not the voice of God. It may be your own voice, it may the voice of a deceiving spirit that you've let come in to you, but God's word says *"Thou shalt not commit adultery".*' If that person had applied this test honestly for themselves, they would not have been deceived.

So when someone comes to you pastorally in the situation outlined above, you've got to say 'forget it, you're in cloud cuckoo-land, it doesn't agree with the Word of God. It isn't God. Leave your life of sin.'

Does it produce the fruit of the Spirit?

Does it release love, joy, peace, goodness and righteousness and all the fruit of the Spirit?

There is something very important that I want to say here. God is moving in a wonderful way amongst young people, and they are always very responsive to change. They can easily receive the message of this book and they will say 'Great, I want to hear God.' This is wonderful, because in their enthusiasm, love and enterprise they will seek God.

They do also need to be showing character change, developing maturity and growing in the knowledge of the Word of God, before I'd actually trust them to be bringing consistently dependable prophecies. I wouldn't want to stop them, I would listen to what they say, but I would be a little cautious about the Christian whether young or old in years, who keeps saying 'God told me this or that.' I believe they can hear God, but I want to see that it is working in them, producing the fruit and changing their character, to know that they are seeking God; before I'm going lay any real weight on what they might bring to the Church. When someone brings a prophetic word in our Church, I always look carefully to see who it is and their quality of life.

Be a clean instrument

We're not playing games. It's fun, it's wonderful to feel that God is speaking to you. But it's awesome, because He's God. In the Old Testament if the prophets didn't hear correctly, if the words didn't come true, they were seen as false prophets and were stoned. So there was a tremendous sense of awe and responsibility with it.

God is a God of grace, and we are living in New Testament times when the gift of prophecy does not carry such dire consequences if misused. God wants us to be bold and eager to be used. But if we are going to be serious we have to come to God as a clean instrument, and if on a Sunday you are coming into your Church and you're saying 'Lord, use me' then come clean and prepared, ready to be a channel for God to speak through. You can't do that if you're rushing in two minutes before the service starts, and you've been watching a video half way through the night on the Saturday night, and your home is in a state of chaos. What is the condition of the instrument, and what is the quality of word you are likely to bring in that situation?

Charles was brought up in a Brethren family. I didn't come out of a 'churchy' background, but when I was married I came into this Brethren situation and in many ways rebelled against the rigidity of it all. But I look back now and I see that there were principles at work which I can fully honour.

In the house of my parents-in-law on Saturday night they had their Bibles open and they were seeking the Lord – not in a heavy way, but it was a quiet evening for them, because they wanted to be sharp instruments to hear the voice of God the next day. In that particular brand of Brethren, and I think it's probably true of most of them, the Sunday morning Breaking of Bread meeting, was the key meeting of the week and was basically for 'Hearing God'. It was an opportunity for the moving of the Spirit. They had never embraced the gifts of the Spirit, but the sensitivity to hear the voice of God and only do what the Lord had told them to do was there. So they prepared themselves.

I want to say to you, whenever you meet corporately as the Body of Christ, go prepared. Go saying, 'Lord, here I am, use me; I'm your instrument, play on me; I'm your channel, flow through me.'

Be a willing instrument

There is another factor that can have an effect on the flowing of the gifts. It is when there are people around who are more experienced than you in using prophetic gifts. I had to cope with this when we lived at the Hyde. It would be all to easy to say 'oh, Colin Urquhart's here, the Lord will speak through him.' There is a sense in which we all do that. But keep your ears open because God could very well choose to speak through you.

I would always, in that situation, be honouring the experience that I know is there in the meeting, but not be in fear of it and not standing so far back that I can't say 'God, you can use me.' I know that part of that is a growing in experience. But I remember many years ago being in a meeting with Don Double. I was filled with the Holy Spirit, it was in the days when I heard the Lord, but I wasn't very confident that I always heard Him. This particular night in a meeting in Truro, I had a very strong impression that the Lord wanted to speak a prophecy through me, but out of fear, out of a sense that there were more experienced people there, I did not bring the word that I had. Afterwards, as we were clearing up, I said to Don 'the Lord gave me a word tonight but I didn't bring it.' His reaction surprised me greatly. He rounded on me, as only Don can, all 6′ 7″ of him, and he said to me 'if you withhold the Word of God from the Body, it's a lack of love; if the Spirit of God is saying something to you and you don't give it, it's a lack of love for your brethren.' And he put me on the spot and said, 'why didn't you give it?' I had to say that really it was the fear of being rejected, it was the fear of being foolish; I thought 'perhaps I might get it wrong, perhaps somebody might rebuke me publicly and make me look stupid.'

There were many reasons why I withheld bringing a prophecy to that meeting, but I learned a lesson that essentially I had made all those reasons bigger than my love for God and for the people.

If you trust the leadership in the meeting, then you ought to be able to trust that they will stop you if you need to be stopped, gently correct you if you need to be corrected (probably afterwards), and teach you and train you in the use of the gift of prophecy, if they see you're inexperienced. But you must still give it.

Now, that almost sounds like a contradiction to what I was saying concerning new Christians. But please hear my heart, because I believe there are two different things here. There's the over-enthusiasm of the inexperienced, and there's the hanging-back of the diffident. I believe there are lots of people who can hear the Lord but hold back for many different reasons. However, essentially you need to 'follow the way of love'. If your motive in bringing the word is love and the building up of the Body you will not go far wrong.

Let's summarise some of the reasons why we keep our mouths shut:
- the fear of being wrong;
- the fear that we might misrepresent the Lord;
- the fear of appearing foolish.

None of these should stop you bringing what you've heard if you feel it passes the tests I've given above. Your job is to bring the Word, the job of the Body is to test it. So once you've given what you believe the Lord has told you to give, it's the job of the Body to test it and to receive it and it's the job of the leadership to affirm it or not.

Chapter 11

The Role of Leadership

When God spoke to His people in Old Testament times, He spoke very plainly. As I've said, being the prophet was an awesome responsibility, so the prophet was in general pretty sure about his message before he brought it! There were false prophets, of course, but the scriptures are very clear who had the word of the Lord and who hadn't. In the gospels, God spoke through angels, through individuals such as Mary and Simeon, and then through Jesus. What they brought were major prophecies, landmarks, and there was no disputing them.

But when we come into the Acts, and to the writings of Paul and the story of the young church, we find a different story. God is using people – ordinary people – to bring his messages. They're all hearing Him. And soon there's disorder. There's chaos. There's a whole mix-up of human failings and muddle and riotous goings-on; because human beings are enthusiastic and messy and muddled. And Paul has to write to the Corinthians, for instance, and lay down the ground-rules for them. He says, in 1 Corinthians 14:40,

> *'Everything should be done in a fitting and orderly way.'*

That's an instruction for us just as much as it was for them.

So how do we do it? All the rules of thumb I've already given for individual listening apply here too. But there's more, because in a body of, say, twenty people, you can have twenty pairs of ears all trying to hear what God is saying, and twenty mouths all trying to pass it on. We need a leader, someone who is submitted to the Holy Spirit, humble, sensitive and obedient, and following the way of love. We need people who are submitted to the Holy Spirit and to the leader, humble, sensitive and obedient, willing to let the leader lead them. Then there will be an atmosphere of peace, joy, trust and order in the meeting.

Each meeting may be entirely different in content; but there's a basic structure which has to be working in harmony. The Holy Spirit must be the boss. The leader must be listening to the Spirit and willing to be a channel through whom the Spirit can bless the people. His top priority must be to please the Spirit and not to grieve Him. The praise and worship leaders will be working under the overall leader to bring the people into the presence of God. The people need to be willing to follow, and to be open channels for God to use.

I really want to emphasise that humility is vital. When pride is there saying 'hear me, hear me, this is the word of the Lord, I'm bringing you the word of the Lord,' I find an in-built resistance in me which makes it very hard to receive what is being said, because I discern it is coming from a wrong spirit. But if it's coming from a teachable spirit, then you can have confidence that it's going to be a good and reliable word.

Lead, don't crush

I have a word of caution here for those of you who are in leadership. Paul said *'I wish that everybody would prophesy, I wish that all God's people would be prophets.'* But we do need to be cautious about how much weight we attach to prophecy. You can see the danger with somebody who is inexperienced and enthusiastic; if you too readily give them the floor and say 'that is a word from the Lord' they may well bring more and more, and very soon they are puffed up and proud and they are saying 'I am the prophet.' Have you met those kind of folk? I am sure that some of you have. Just be careful.

There is an awesome responsibility with hearing God.

I believe that leaders should train people in using the gifts of the Spirit; they mustn't crush them. God never does that. He always encourages. If He corrects, He always shows you where you went wrong; if you think you have made a fool of yourself, He will always give you a doorway of hope, another opportunity to get it right. A leader must respect and care for the people even as he corrects them.

Detecting the flesh

As I've said earlier, there will be a mixture of the human and the divine in all prophetic utterances. I remember the example of a young woman in our church who recently brought a prophetic word, it began well and we could discern that God was speaking, but she just didn't know how to end and went on too long. I could actually sense when the Spirit of God stopped speaking and when she continued trying to bring the word to a conclusion.

I went to her later, and said 'I want to encourage you, the first part of that word you brought was spot on, it was good, be encouraged. But you didn't know when to stop and the second part was you.' She looked a bit sheepish and admitted that I was right. I hope I wasn't too heavy-handed, but she needed to hear it. I don't think she resented it, in fact I know she didn't, because she has grown in her use of the gifts since then.

Detecting and avoiding repetition

When we first start hearing the Lord, we're often so eager to be used by Him, it's such a new-found joy, that we are in danger of listening to the preaching and the contributions of others, and then repeating the gist of what we have heard, turning it into a sort of prophecy.

I remember at the time when we were working with Colin in the Bethany Fellowship, we had a new man come to join us. Our daily practice was to have a time of worship and waiting on the Lord each morning. We would sing, then it was usually Colin who would bring a message from Scripture, after which we would listen to the Lord, and speak out any prophetic words that we were hearing.

Almost every day this guy would speak a word that

merely summarised what Colin had already spoken. This grated on me, because I thought 'all he's doing is repeating what Colin has said in his message and bringing it out as "thus saith the Lord", he's not saying anything new.' I became very irritated by this because what he was doing seemed so obvious to me.

There was nothing wrong in what he was saying, except that we had heard it already, and it didn't need saying again. In the end I went to Colin and said 'I know this sounds critical, but this is driving me mad. Rebuke me if I'm wrong, and I'll go and sort myself out, but if he's doing what I think he is doing, why don't you stop him?'

Colin said, 'you're right, he is doing what you say, and I know it, but don't worry about it. I could crush him, I could jump on him from a great height and say "shut up"; or I can let it continue believing that as he gets more secure he won't need to do it any more.' As time went by and he became more safe in the love of the fellowship the problem did, indeed, solve itself.

A similar situation can arise when there are a lot of prophetic words being given in a meeting which seem to be saying similar things, but in slightly different words. At one level this is encouraging, because it shows that God's message to the Church is being heard by many of the people; however it can blur the issue. I well remember Charles needing to speak to his Leaders Week team about this problem, during the days when we were living at the Hyde and he was training them in using the gifts. He said, 'when you hear someone giving a prophetic word which is very close to what you are hearing, just say "Hallelujah" inside, you don't need to repeat it in slightly different words.' Those doing this are often so excited they are in harmony with what God is saying, they want to tell everyone, 'I heard it too,' which literally is an expression of pride. It does need to be controlled, because the constant repetition of the same concepts brings confusion not clarity.

Practicalities

In our church, Charles is usually leading the meeting, and we encourage those people who are hearing prophetic words to come to him and whisper the gist of the word, vision, or whatever has prophetically been given them by the Lord. At that point their responsibility ends. It's up to Charles then to judge how and when the contribution fits into the overall flow of the meeting. Sometimes he can make mistakes, just as we can in what we bring. But if we trust each other, no serious harm results. Often a word is brought at the right time and can be given at once. At other times, Charles may say, 'just hang on a minute, this is not the right moment for your word.' Later he may well call up that person to the microphone to bring their contribution, which will be at a time he feels more appropriate. Sometimes Charles will say, 'leave that word with me' – because he discerns that it isn't in harmony with the meeting or it's almost the same as has been said in the last two prophecies.

Holding on to the message

When there have been a number of the prophetic words or pictures, Charles will summarise the various strands of what has been said, gather them all together, remind the people what the Lord has been saying, and then apply it to the Church, so that there can be a response of faith and action.

I find that people forget prophetic words very quickly. It's good therefore to have somebody in the Church with a very good memory, who can write down on a meeting-by-meeting basis a short synopsis of what the Lord's been saying. This enables the Church to consider these at regular intervals and see if the right action has been taken. There is a danger in receiving so much that we do not take it seriously or obey God's directives.

Dealing with 'words' for individuals

In the next chapter I will be dealing with the way prophecy is tested in Church. However, one of the dangers of encouraging the whole Church to use the gifts of the Holy Spirit is when people start receiving prophetic words for other people. I have known some who go absolutely crazy and think they have a word for everybody; they soon think they are the prophet to the church and also to everybody else. They go around, driving everybody mad saying 'I've got a word from the Lord for you,' or, 'as I was listening to the Lord this morning He said this to me about you.' Have you experienced that?

When God speaks I think you need to ask Him:
– 'Is this for me?'
– 'Is this for the Church Body?'

If you have a sense that it's for somebody else, be very careful before you go and give it. Just ask the Lord to make the timing absolutely right, and make you very sensitive and gentle as you give that word.

You may well ask, 'if that person is the Lord's child then why doesn't He speak to him directly? Why does He need me?' I believe that there is an important principle here; any word that you bring to someone else, who is sensitive to God's voice, will only confirm that which they are already hearing from God.

And sometimes we're bringing words to people which come out of our concern for them, our observation of them, rather than divine revelation, and in which there's an awful lot of 'us'. Be very watchful for that tendency.

This practice, if discovered going on in your Church, must be stopped, because it can cause much trouble. It is the opposite extreme from 'we don't do it because we are too afraid of getting it wrong.' Suddenly we think 'I can do this' and we go crazy, pride emerges, and out of our pride we think we've got to give words to everybody. These are the dangers at the two ends of the spectrum.

I'll give you an example – we had a lady in our church who was feeling somewhat neglected, and therefore was being critical; no-one was doing quite what she wanted them to do and she was having a 'beef' about everyone. So I said to her, 'you ask the Lord about it, don't moan to me, hear what God is saying.' When she began to listen, she was given a picture of a person with hands cut off at the wrists, which she interpreted as the Lord saying to her 'My Body has got its hands cut off,' and so she began to go round saying 'you know what's wrong, the Church is the Body of Christ, but it's got its hands cut off, and that's why nobody is actually ministering to anybody's needs.'

She applied it to people other than herself as it

confirmed what she already thought about her Church. As she shared this with one of the people in the Church, she was asked, 'if God gave you that word, don't you think He was speaking to you about it? What are you doing about it? In what way are **you** the hands of Jesus, where are **you** reaching out, what are **you** doing?' She came to see that this other person was right. It is important that first of all we apply the word to ourselves.

Now it was true that the Church also needed to hear that word, because we always need stirring up in our caring, loving and the way we minister to people. But she was about to side-step the word and say 'well, this is the Word of the Lord for the Church' and take herself out of line. When people do that, we need to push them back on track and say 'if God gave it to you, He's speaking to you first, you deal with what it says; and then it may be that you'll need to share it with the Body at a later date and say "Yes, God said this to me and I did this", but perhaps He needs to also say it to you.'

Chapter 12

Test Everything –
Hold on to the Good

Paul had these instructions for the believers at Thessalonika,

> 'Do not put out the Spirit's fire; do not treat prophecies with contempt. Test everything. Hold on to the good. Avoid every kind of evil.'
> (1 Thessalonians 5:19–22)

When Paul was instructing the Corinthians, he told them that when the prophets were speaking, the others should weigh carefully what was being said (1 Corinthians 14:29).

Paul also states that when God gives you something, you can hold it. You don't have to speak it out immediately, you can keep it in your spirit. He put it this way,

> 'The spirits of prophets are subject to the control of prophets. For God is not a God of disorder, but of peace.'
> (1 Corinthians 14:32–33)

There is however encouragement for everyone to join in, as Paul describes here,

> *'For you can all prophesy in turn so that everybody may be instructed and encouraged.'*
> (1 Corinthians 14:31)

When we have received a prophetic word, we can weigh that word, we can sit on that word, until we believe it is the right moment to bring it in an orderly and godly way.

We always have to remember that prophetic words are not on the same level as Scripture. The Bible, The Word of God, is the living Word of God. The Holy Bible that you have in your possession are the scriptures given by inspiration of the Holy Spirit. Don't ever put anything above it.

We had a very sad situation in our own church recently which we've had to deal with pastorally. A lovely man, much loved, went to be with the Lord recently. He had discovered a cancerous growth in his lymphatic glands, and even though we as a Church prayed and wrestled and believed that the Lord would raise him up, the Lord chose to take him to himself. We don't fully understand all the reasons, but we can rejoice to know that he's with the Lord.

However, his wife had a collection of prophetic words that had been given to them over the years; her chief problem was not that the Lord had taken her husband, but with the fact that these prophetic words had not been fulfilled. We had to spend quite a lot of time with her looking at them, trying to discern whether they had come from the Lord, and how were they to be interpreted? Sometimes we interpret prophecy how we want to interpret it.

When we looked together at one prophecy in particular, we saw that she had interpreted it to apply to the here and now, when in fact, when read again, it quite clearly referred to the hereafter. When she saw this she was released from the misunderstanding.

But it awakened in me the sense of the danger of giving prophetic words to people, which are received as if they were the Word of God. Those people are then waiting for that word to be fulfilled, and if it does not occur, it causes terrible disappointment, and can undermine their confidence in God. We want to hear prophetic words from the Lord, but the only thing which is irrefutable is the Bible, the Word of God, because prophecy is imperfect. So be careful and test everything.

When Scripture says *'test everything'*, it doesn't mean be unbelieving, it means 'be wise, be discerning'. Test it, don't just receive it as if it's Scripture. The Bible is the Gospel, it is rock solid, it is what the Word of God says you can trust because every promise is 'Amen in Jesus' and He will fulfil every promise that He has made. Not one promise has ever been broken that the Word of God has made to you.

The foremost person who must test what's being given is, again, the leader. Therefore, the leader needs to be mature and have spiritual authority, and to be one step ahead of everybody else, because he is responsible for hearing what the Spirit of God is saying to that whole meeting and has to keep focused on what is important.

As the Spirit of God is speaking, and people are bringing pictures, visions, prophetic words, prophetic scriptures, the leader above all has got to have his ears open saying 'Lord, what are the important things you're saying here? What are the things we can perhaps leave and look at through a preached word later on? What do we need to hear to-day? What is the subject that you're opening up and saying "Look at this, Church"?'

Hold on to what is good, be prepared to correct and be prepared to stop if necessary.

Correcting

I've been in meetings where things have been said which have been absolutely out of order. I can remember a big meeting in London when somebody brought a prophetic word which my spirit immediately told me was off-beam. Suddenly, the leader of the meeting said 'take that man out' which jarred in my spirit even more, as I felt the poor fellow would be so crushed, embarrassed and put down by it; and as far as I was concerned that was the end of the meeting for me because it was wrongly handled. I remember a situation in our own church when a visitor came and brought a prophetic word.

As this visitor began to speak I knew in my spirit he needed to be stopped. The first few sentences were in the Spirit but very soon I had a sense that he was wanting to take the place over. Charles was leading the meeting and he walked out to the front, very purposefully, and put his arm around him. You could feel the relief in the people, because if you have a spiritually sensitive Body they know what's going on, and they are expecting the leadership to get in there and keep control.

Charles put his arm around this brother as he waited for him to finish his sentence, interrupted and said 'thank you' loudly, strongly and authoritatively, then said 'well, brother, it's good to have you with us, and thank you for what you've brought, but we'll move on now.' He then prayed and gently guided him back in the right direction towards where he had been sitting.

Now the spiritual people in the meeting were saying 'thank you, Lord.' The people who had no discernment were not offended, because the brother had not been embarrassed, he was not made to look stupid, he was affirmed because he had an arm around him, but there was no uncertainty, he knew he had to sit down.

It is important, when you are agreeing in prayer before the meeting starts, to pray that the Holy Spirit and only the Holy Spirit will be in control. When you do open things up there's always the danger that somebody will either say too much or something with which you're not happy.

It is important that we test everything; those in the Church need to know that we are weighing carefully every contribution and if there are those who are not willing to come under authority like that then they won't be permitted to function within the Church.

Chapter 13

The Word that Sets the Captives Free

Listening to God has an essential part to play when you are involved in personal counselling. This is an area where I feel it's imperative that we are confident in hearing the voice of God.

Apart from other considerations, it saves a great deal of time when you have to see somebody. Perhaps they ring you up and say 'will you pray with me? I need to see you.' It could be a stranger or it may be somebody known to you, if it's in a church situation. If you will spend some time before you meet together to go to the Lord and say, 'will you speak to me about this situation, tell me what I need to know,' you'll find that you do not become involved in a long and wearisome session. Because, if you hear from God, He will tell you details about the situation which can by-pass the lengthy time it often takes for people to become comfortable and off-load their whole story.

If you are experienced in counselling, you will know what I'm talking about. Sometimes people don't know where to start, they tell you their life story and it may take two hours before they get to the point that is pertinent to their need. But, if you've already gone to the Lord and asked Him to speak, He can fill in those details before they come, or He can tell you just what is going to be pertinent.

Saving time

I remember a situation in Sweden when a girl, who had a very violent past, came to the conference where Charles and I were speaking. Only days before she had attacked her parents with a broken bottle. She came to Charles on the Saturday night and asked for prayer; he had the sense that she needed to come under the word of God and be at every meeting until the middle of the following week. This was to be a preparation before we ministered to her, because we wanted her to receive the Word and spend time in an atmosphere of worship, before we actually started probing the problem, as we knew it had a demonic source, and we also knew there was a lot of violence attached to it.

When it came to the Wednesday, Charles said to me 'I think you ought to speak to her.' So I went to the Lord and said 'now, Lord, will you speak to me about this situation?'

He said something very interesting to me; 'don't let her talk.' Very strange. He then described her situation to me, in fact He gave me a synopsis of her life and background. Not the precise details, but the general principles. He told me that she had been a very clever girl, but that she had used that cleverness to manipulate. I also learned that she had never had enough love, and she had always sought to cause trouble in her family because in that way she received the attention she wanted. She was always craving for love, and this latest behaviour was attention-seeking at a much greater level.

Then He repeated, 'don't let her speak, just tell her everything I've told you.' I thought, 'Lord, that's going to be quite hard.' When I met with her, I found that she was a Swedish girl who spoke very good English, which is not uncommon in Sweden; I did however have the pastor's wife with me in case there was any difficulty with the language. She came in and sat down, was just about to tip everything out on me, when I said to her 'wait a minute, God spoke to me in a very strange way when I was praying for you, and He told me that you weren't to speak, just to listen.' I then gently proceeded to tell her what the Lord had told me.

She began to cry and cry. I knew I had hit the right spot. I knew, too, that God had done it like that because she was not a Christian, and she needed to know that God knew her and saw her. That, in fact, created faith in her that God could do something about the problem.

The pastor's wife and I then began to minister to her; 'God can set you free, we can set you free in the Name of Jesus now, but we can't keep you free unless you invite the power of God to come into you, which will heal you up and set your life on a new course, and that's your choice. We can pray for you, we can set you free, but unless you choose freedom as a life-style by inviting Jesus to be the Lord of your life, you will not remain free.'

Then she began to talk and talk, and as I was trying to get a word in edgeways (and I'm quite good at getting a word in edgeways!), I realised why the Lord had told me not to let her talk. We would have been there for days. But because God had been so specific we had been able to deal with the problem. I learned a lesson in that – to always go to the Lord and say 'tell me what I need to know.' I can't remember another time when He's told me so much in specific terms or told me to keep anybody quiet. But He knew what He was doing then. We must be prepared to do what God says.

Reaching the buried truth

At another time, a man came to me with a very difficult situation. He told me traumatic things, and when you're counselling you listen carefully, but in two different ways at once. People tell you things at a natural level, but what's really in their heart is so painful that they find it difficult to put into words and they don't quite know how to tell you. So you must keep listening naturally, while at the same time opening your spiritual ears, in fact listening at two levels simultaneously.

I have a very keen sense of smell. This is natural for me, and I drive my family mad because they think I'm a bloodhound, I can always smell things before anybody else. But now suddenly the smell of flour filled the room, or that is how it seemed to me, just the dusty smell of grain.

This dusty smell was so impressed upon me that I stopped him and said, 'look, this might seem the strangest thing in the world, but I've just got this incredible sense of the smell of flour. Did any of these things that have hurt you so much happen in a dusty, floury place?' Immediately, he broke down and began to sob uncontrollably.

That was the break-through point, for from that moment he was able to open up and tell me that he had been raped when he was in the merchant navy in a grain-store on board ship. He had never told anyone before. This had happened when he had been a young man and had been at the source of all his problems, but he had never been able to speak it out. Now, the Spirit of God was speaking to me, but He didn't say 'grain store', He didn't even say 'rape', He just gave me the sense of smell, because, in fact, it was the gentlest way of opening up the situation.

So be prepared for the unusual. It's hearing God, but it's perhaps not what you would expect, it certainly was not what I would have expected in that situation. If you're following the way of love, sometimes God will actually tell you to do something which you would recoil from and say 'strange'.

Touching the heart

At another time, I'd spent a number of hours with a lady, who I didn't know very well, and I wasn't getting very far. I knew we weren't reaching the real issues. I just felt all the time that I wasn't touching her, that there was a large barrier.

I stopped her and said 'look, we've talked a long time, let's just pray. I need to hear what God's saying to me.' As we turned to prayer, God gave me a picture of a cat. He just filled my mind with this cat. It wasn't the ordinary, creamy coloured Siamese, it was a brown cat and it had a funny tail.

Now, I knew nothing about cats, so I just said to her 'I can't hear anything from the Lord at the moment, but I keep getting a picture of this cat,' and described it, whereupon she just started to weep in deep loud wails, and I knew that this must mean something to her. By the time she stopped crying and we were able to talk again, she told me that she had two of these particular cats, which are actually Burmese and quite rare, and I had accurately described her own cats to her.

It had opened the door, it had broken down the barrier. Then I continued listening to the Lord. I said 'you love those cats very much don't you?' 'Yes, I do, and they love me,' she said. 'I think they are the only things in the world that love me.'

Then I said to her 'you have been telling me that you don't know how to love, because you've never received love, but you do know how to love because you love your cats. Now God loves you far more than you love your cats.' And that was what she needed to hear. That broke through and the counselling session soon ended. God gave me that picture, because there was no other way that I could have communicated the love of God to her. In human terms she had not experienced love. But she did have it in her heart, it might be for cats, but it was love. And somehow, I can't tell you all the details, but that strange picture of a funny cat with a funny tail was used by God to communicate His voice into her spirit, and set her free to be the person God wanted her to become.

Now, I can't tell you why God chooses to do things the way He does; I only know that God is utterly creative and He will give people pictures. He will do things in a way which will minister to them uniquely, and in a way that they can understand and that they will never forget, because of His love for His children. She'll never forget, even if I don't see her this side of eternity, that when she was sitting in my sitting room one day, God showed me a picture of her two cats, and communicated His love to her in that very intimate way. So I want to encourage you to be open to the Spirit of God.

Find the root

There are times in the pastoral ministry that we're seeking to deal with things that we can't seem to reach. If you have experienced this you will know what I'm talking about; people have problems, you've explored everything you know in terms of your own knowledge in order to get to the root of the problem and yet you're aware that you're dealing with something you have not been able to reach.

You may find these scriptures helpful. One of them is Daniel 2:22 – it's the story of when the king has a dream which he is unwilling to recount, he says to Daniel and his friends 'you'll die unless you tell me the dream and the interpretation.'

That sounds crazy, but Daniel prays and he fasts and he gets his friends with him to fast, and then *'during the night the mystery was revealed to Daniel in a vision.'* Verse 22 says, and it's talking about God,

> *'He reveals deep and hidden things; He knows what lies in darkness, and light dwells with Him.'*

When you're up against that sort of problem, it isn't the unwillingness of the person to tell you what it is, it's perhaps so locked in their memory that they have no idea what the source of the problem is. Then pray, fast, gather together a group of people who are experienced in listening to God and actually ask God to reveal what lies in darkness; it's part of carrying each other's burdens.

Look at Job 36:8:

> *'If men are bound in chains, held fast by cords of affliction, He (God) tells them what they have done – that they have sinned arrogantly. He makes them listen to correction and commands them to repent of their evil. If they obey and serve Him they will spend the rest of their days in prosperity and their years in contentment. But if they do not listen, they will perish by the sword and die without knowledge.'*

Again, this verse gives us a sense that if people do really want to know what is at the heart of the problem, God will show them.

Double check

I would sound a warning bell here. When God reveals that hidden thing to you, and you communicate it to the person to whom you are ministering, they will immediately have an inner witness that you have received it from God. It may even open up their memory so that they can again recall it from their own past. If there is no flicker of response to the word you have received, you need to go back to God again, and not try and push through with your revelation; you may have heard wrongly.

Know when to keep silent

Whenever God gives you an insight into the hearts and minds of men and women, you are not there to judge or to talk about it, but to pray. We do too much talking about what we see. But when God pulls back the curtain of heaven and He shows you something, get on your knees and intercede; He's showing you for a purpose. He may well be showing you so that at some time you can deal with it in that person because you have knowledge; but initially, pray. Take the revelational knowledge that God gives you and pray, until God gives you directions as to what you are to do.

Sometimes I know that I can see things; a problem, a difficulty, and I have understanding as to the source of it. In the past I would go in where angels fear to tread, I would crash in and do a lot of damage. I've learned a bit of wisdom since then, and I know when God shows me things I must wait until the Holy Spirit says 'now's the moment.'

In Jeremiah 23, God is speaking to Jeremiah about false prophets, but nonetheless they are interesting verses which we can apply to ourselves.

> *'Which of them has stood in the council of the LORD to see or hear His word? Who has listened and heard His word?'* (Jeremiah 23:18)

And in verse 22,

> *'If they had stood in my council they would have proclaimed my words to my people and would have*

*turned them from their evil ways and from their
evil deeds.'*

Now hear that cry from the heart of God again, 'If
only my people would have come and listened.' The
effect of it would be righteousness. Because if you go
on to verses 28 and 29 it says,

> ' *"Let the prophet who has a dream, tell his dream
> but let the one who has my word speak it faithfully.
> For what has straw to do with grain?" declares the
> LORD. "Is not my word like fire," declares the
> LORD "and like a hammer that breaks a rock in
> pieces?"* '

I want to tell you that when you hear the word of the
Lord and you apply it to a situation, it will be like a
hammer that breaks the rock in pieces. And the more
we do it, the more accurate we will be in the use of
that hammer, so it breaks just what needs to be
broken but doesn't crush.

The New Testament assumes we will be part of the
Body of Christ, the living church, and therefore under
authority, regularly worshipping, receiving teaching
and accountable to our brothers and sisters in the
Lord. This is a place of safety and security. God
desires that we individually are led by the Spirit of
God.

> *'Those who are led by the Spirit of God are sons of
> God.'*   (Romans 8:14)

He desires that we collectively represent Him as we
love each other, live in harmony, according to His

written Word, and are in a place where we each receive correction; where we live in a family – the family of God.

We look back into church history and see that people who began well living as Christians and then came out of the Body were deceived and led astray; sometimes so proud and convinced of their rightness that no-one could help and lead them back into reality. To-day there are sadly also people who will not admit they could be wrong about what they have heard and persist in believing they are right and everyone else who disagrees with them is wrong and against them.

If we march with a thousand men and only one is out of step it is reasonable to assume the 999 have got it right and the one is wrong. But sometimes the 'out of step' one will be utterly convinced they are the persecuted minority with the world against them.

Let's avoid such behaviour as we seek to hear God. Let's be filled with the Spirit.

> *'Be very careful, then, how you live – not as unwise but as wise, making the most of every opportunity, because the days are evil. Therefore do not be foolish, but understand what the Lord's will is. Do not get drunk on wine, which leads to debauchery. Instead, be filled with the Spirit. Speak to one another with psalms, hymns and spiritual songs. Sing and make music in your heart to the Lord, always giving thanks to God the Father for everything, in the name of our Lord Jesus Christ. Submit to one another out of reverence for Christ.'*
> (Ephesians 5:15–21)

Let the word of God dwell in you richly (Colossians 3:16), and do not neglect the assembling of yourselves together (Hebrews 10:25).

Hearing the voice of God is serious business. It is not something to titillate us, it's not the latest gimmick, it might be life and death for somebody that you're ministering to. If we as the Body are going to carry each others' burdens, if we're going to fulfil the Law of Christ, if we're going to walk in the way of love, we need to give ourselves to knowing surely that we can hear the voice of God.

Chapter 14

You Can Hear God

In this final chapter I want to share a testimony of how my daughter, Joanna, began to launch out in speaking out the things which she was hearing from God. It has always been a principle of our lives that when Charles goes out in ministry, he does not go alone. Many times I am able to accompany him but when our children were growing up this was not possible. It was some years ago now when Charles was travelling to Austria and Hungary and, as our daughter Joanna was working in Germany for a Christian organisation, we enquired as to whether it would be possible for her to go with Charles to be a companion and prayer support to him. This was a great joy to them both and Jo was thrilled to be with her father, but there was a certain reticence – 'will I be sensitive enough to the Holy Spirit to be a real support to Dad?'

During the time in Hungary Charles was invited to speak to a meeting of pastors; this was during the Communist era and the meeting for pastors needed to be moved from place to place so as not to cause suspicion from the authorities. Early in the morning

Charles and Jo left their hotel and were driven many miles out into the countryside where a group of about 30 pastors were meeting together in the home of a reformed church pastor. At the morning session Charles brought some teaching that God had given to him; there was a tremendous response and God was clearly moving in the lives of the pastors. As lunch time approached Charles was seeking God for the afternoon's message when the leader of the group stood up in front of the pastors and made an announcement: 'This afternoon, after we have had lunch, we are inviting Charles to lay his hands on us and pray over us and bring each of us a prophetic word from the Lord.' It was the first Charles had heard of this and it took him completely by surprise. There had been times in the past when God had clearly told him to bring prophetic words into the lives of church leaders, but it wasn't a routine. So the lunch time was spent in earnest seeking of God, so that there might be a real anointing from heaven on this time.

After lunch the pastors regrouped again and one by one they sat down and Charles laid his hands on them and began to speak prophetic words over them. After about the second or third pastor, Jo interrupted and said: 'Dad, I think God is showing me something,' so Charles told her to speak out what God was saying. Each time a wonderfully clear yet simple prophetic word was spoken into the life of one of the pastors. She didn't have a word for all of them, but Charles could see that she was beginning to grow in confidence and at various intervals there would be a tentative, and humble, interruption from Jo saying, 'I think God is saying something to me for this one.'

Undoubtedly a tense moment had arrived as a certain pastor sat in the chair in front of Charles; it was quite obvious that this man was in great need, his life evidently in crisis, and quite clearly the gathered company knew all about this and were just waiting to hear what God had to say to him. As Charles laid his hands on the man and began to pray and ask God's blessing on the man's life and ministry, once again Joanna interjected. 'I think that God is showing me a picture' and she then began to describe a picture of a garden with weeds and brambles, she explained how God was showing the owner of the garden how he needed to get in among those brambles and weeds and cut them down because God's purposes were that the garden should grow things of beauty, flowers and vegetables, where the brambles and weeds had been allowed to grow. There was a gasp in the room as Jo spoke these words. Here was a young girl in her late teens bringing a word from God, which so accurately described this man's situation, that everybody in the room was utterly amazed.

This was the highlight of the whole ministry trip and was the very first thing that Charles told me when he returned. I trust that it will demonstrate to you that you do not need to have attained any great age or depth of experience to be a listener to the voice of God and to hear Him speak clearly into your life and situation. For Jo it was a break-through; she had been encouraged to listen to God as she was brought up in our home, but this was the moment when she stepped out in faith, spoke out what she heard from God and was used by Him to bring a life-changing message to a man who had been in ministry for many, many years and who, in the natural, she would probably feel unqualified to say anything to. But when God speaks we need to listen and when God has something important to say He will choose any person whose heart is willing and open to receive and act upon what they hear.

Now it's time for you to begin to hear God.